A City at War

The 4th Black Watch, 'Dundee's Own', February 1915-March 1916

Julie S. Danskin

Number 54
Dundee
2013

ISBN 978-0-900019-51-7

Printed by Winter & Simpson, Dundee
(01382) 813813

The day you marched away,
Dundee's Own,
Our hearts were like to break,
Dundee's Own.
But you smiled away our tears,
And we stifled all our fears,
Changing them to ringing cheers
For Dundee's Own.

- Anon., 'Dundee's Own',
The People's Journal,
11 December 1915

For the 'Fourth'

Contents

List of Illustrations

List of Abbreviations

BEF   = British Expeditionary Force

BWRA = The Black Watch Regimental Archive

Courier = *The Courier and Argus*, Dundee edition

DORA = Defence of the Realm Act, 1914

Acknowledgements

This publication constitutes the culmination of work done during my undergraduate degree in History at the University of Dundee. My interest in the human experience of the First World War was first sparked at the age of fifteen, when I visited the graveyards and poppy-scattered battlegrounds on the Ypres Salient with my school. This continued throughout my university career and into the present day, so naturally I was delighted when the Abertay Historical Society not only gave me the honour of their Annual Prize for best dissertation on a local topic, but also made the decision to turn my dissertation into a book.

The transformation of this work from undergraduate dissertation to book form has allowed me to follow up fascinating avenues that had to be neglected in the final product submitted to the University due to length restrictions. A particularly important addition is what now constitutes a biographical chapter on the officers' lives, allowing the reader an insight into unpicking the networks and composition of the 4th Black Watch, a valuable and I think crucial way to understand the experiences and viewpoints of these men.

The initial research leading to the production of my dissertation was generously funded by the Carnegie Trust for the Universities of Scotland, which allowed me to trawl through countless newspapers and, happily, to photocopy copious pages much to the dismay of the diligent staff at Dundee Central Library, whom I wish to thank for their toleration of my incessant requests for newspaper volumes. I also wish to thank Mr William Longair for the kind loan of materials from years of personal research, an asset which greatly assisted me from the outset. I have an especial debt to the inimitable Mr Thomas Smyth, the archivist of The Black Watch Regimental Archives for his help and, far more impressively, his patience. Dr William Kenefick has always been on hand to offer advice about the directions my work might take, which is greatly appreciated. Thanks are also owed to Dr Derek Patrick, the supervisor of my undergraduate dissertation, for editorial help to transition my work to book form. I would also like to thank the Secretary of the Abertay Historical Society, Matthew Jarron, for his meticulous close-readings of the text, his design for the front cover, and for his excellent advice more generally. Finally, I have the utmost gratitude towards Sir Alistair Irwin, the Chairman of the Trustees of The Black Watch Regimental Museum, both for his sparkling correspondence and for providing such a wonderful foreword to this book.

On a personal note, I wish to sincerely thank my parents: Kate Danskin, for her incredible calming influence; and Colin Danskin for producing high-resolution images of Sidney Steven's photographs, which take up the majority of the plate section. Without my family and their unflinching support throughout my degree and beyond, I simply would not know what to do. I would also like to thank Professor Christopher Whatley and Anna Day for mentoring me in the publishing world during my time working for Dundee University Press, which has made this project infinitely easier. I'd also like to thank Alissa Jones Nelson, Matt Nelson, Fiona Morton, Eddie Small and especially Fiona Meek, for reasons which I hope I have made clear. Particular love and gratitude goes towards my wonderful grandmother Marjorie Batchelor, whose proofreading assured the quality of my undergraduate dissertation back in 2010. Her duties have been diligently passed on to Chris Kydd, who showed so much care and attention in helping me prepare this text for publication. For that, and for so much else, I thank and adore him.

Foreword

by Lieutenant General Sir Alastair Irwin KCB CBE
Chairman of the Trustees of the Black Watch Museum

James and Joan Dick of Morgan Street, Dundee were no doubt amongst the cheering crowds as the men of the 4th Battalion The Black Watch entrained at Tay Bridge Station on 23 February 2015, heading for Southampton and the ship that would take them to the war in France. Barely three weeks later their son, Corporal Ralph Dick, became the first man of the 4th Battalion to be killed in action. He was buried where he fell by his comrades, his grave marked by a wooden cross. During the course of the next three years of fighting his grave was lost and his name is now recorded on the Black Watch panel on the Commonwealth War Graves Memorial at Le Touret a few miles north east of Bethune. Other Dundee families with sons serving in the 1st and 2nd Battalions would already have received the dreaded War Office telegram reporting the worst of all possible news but it was Mr and Mrs Dick who had the sad distinction of being the first Dundonian family to lose a member of the 4th Battalion, not itself a regular infantry unit but a part of the Territorial Army. Their son had gone to war not as a committed professional soldier but as a citizen who had volunteered for part-time military service in peace time and who did not turn his back when he was mobilised to fight for his country. By the time, a year or so later, that the Battalion had been merged with the 5th, 423 officers and men had been killed – all, like Corporal Dick, sons of Dundee, all of them men whose desire to serve their country overcame their fears of what dangers awaited them on the Western Front.

On guard duty in the Dundee area, the 4th Battalion had a slow and unexciting start to the war. Though well trained and respectably if not lavishly equipped the battalion that eventually proceeded to war was untested by battle. The test came soon enough.   Once in France the battalion experienced all the boredoms, discomforts and extreme dangers of trench warfare, those elemental characteristics of the familiar but deadly pattern of the infantry's active service on the western front. The spells in the line took their steady toll of men like

Corporal Dick but it was the great battles of Neuve Chapelle, Aubers Ridge and Loos which between them established the Battalion's indelible reputation for fighting prowess, courage and sacrifice. That sacrifice would have been keenly felt in Dundee where there can have been very few people who did not have a relation or friend in the Battalion, very few who were not in some way affected by the losses suffered by the sons of their city. Yet Dundee's support for its fighting men and the city's resilience and determination in the face of long casualty lists continued undiminished. Invaluable though all this was to the national war effort, the knowledge that the city was so strongly behind them was more valuable still to the Black Watch men at the front, inspiring them as they daily faced the challenges of battle. It would not be an exaggeration to suggest that the achievements of the 4th Battalion at the front were in fact the achievements of Dundee itself.

I was delighted to be asked to provide this preface. My father's maternal family had many associations with the 4th Battalion; himself an officer in The Black Watch he was appointed adjutant of the 4th/5th Battalion in 1947. As a happy consequence of that posting, I am fortunate to be able to boast on my passport that I was born in Dundee. So it is a particular privilege to be able to contribute these few words in honour of Corporal Dick and of all his comrades who did so much to enhance the reputation of their battalion, their regiment and their great city. During the course of its relatively short existence the 4th Battalion forged a fighting reputation second to none. This book, so aptly timed as we approach the centenary of the outbreak of the Great War, tells an inspiring tale that is of as much relevance now as it was at the time, for it reminds Dundonians of what can be achieved and overcome with the character and determination that is so typical of their city.

Introduction
A City at War?

When o' worldly cares I'm free,
And I've crossed the 'sullen sea',
Weel tae the fore I ken I'll see
Lads o' the Fourth.

- W.D.M, 'Oor Gallant Fourth'
The People's Journal, 16 October 1915

The 4th Battalion of The Black Watch was Dundonian to its core. For any soldier, writer or historian, the claim that the Scottish city of Dundee constituted 'a city at war' during the First World War is bold. It suggests a sense of universality and comprehensiveness that is difficult to defend. Nevertheless, two important commentators on the conflict, both of whom experienced battle firsthand, justified this characterisation of Dundee as 'a city at war' in their respective histories of the most famous Scottish Highland regiment: The Black Watch. Both the high-ranking officer Major-General A.G. Wauchope and the famous Scottish writer Eric Linklater – neither of whom were themselves Dundonian – note that the 4th Black Watch, commonly known at the time as 'Dundee's Own', was remarkable as it drew virtually all its recruits directly from the city itself. Indeed, Major-General Wauchope stated outright that 'in the history of the Regiment during the Great War the 4th Battalion holds a notable position, since it represented a Scottish city at war'.[1]

Beyond the 'Fourth', Dundee is notable for its impressive contribution of soldiers to the war effort. Men sent to the various arenas of the First World War certainly did not only belong to the 'Fourth'; nor just to The Black Watch; nor indeed to solely Scottish regiments. Many belonged to British and even colonial regiments. A Dundee newspaper in the 1920s indicated that approximately 63 per cent of the city's adult male population had been invested in the Great War's battlefields.[2] This figure corroborates T.C. Smout's wider theory that Scotland contributed a disproportionate number of recruits to the war of 1914-1918, a fact which has been a cause for both pride and sorrow simultaneously.[3] In Dundee, the focus, particularly in the city's newspapers, revolved around the 4th Battalion as a representative body of the city. Wauchope argued that the experiences of the 'Fourth' in particular influenced and significantly shaped the public opinion of Dundonians who remained at home. However, if the 'Fourth' comprised a relatively small percentage of Dundonians in the wider experience of the First World War, why was so much emphasis placed at home on a small Territorial battalion that survived independently for little over a year?

It should be clarified at the beginning of this book that the term 'Dundee's Own' was not exclusive to the relatively few soldiers belonging to that Territorial battalion, and certainly does not negate the contribution made by Dundonians serving in other regiments. It was called 'Dundee's Own' because it was unique as a voluntary Territorial battalion in The Black Watch in the sense that almost all of its recruits were drawn from the city of Dundee itself; the other Territorial battalions in the regiment recruited more widely from the city's hinterlands in Forfar, Perth and Fife. Wauchope also stated in his brief paragraph on the links between Dundee and her 'own' battalion that 'the Battalion had in it the spirit and local patriotism which is the basis of so much that is best in Scottish character and in Scottish history'.[4] Indeed, the letters and poems that the people of Dundee contributed to local newspapers illustrate that the city's pride and mourning was not restricted to the men of the 4th Black Watch alone. These soldiers were merely the most easily identifiable representatives of the city's part in the war effort. This was stated outright in *The People's Journal*, one of the Dundee newspapers, making its stance clear in the issue celebrating the departure of the 4th Black Watch as it left for France:

> The '4th' represents but a fraction of the men the city has
> contributed for service in the greatest of the world's wars. But in
> a very special sense it is Dundee's regiment and it carries with it
> the honour of the town.[5]

Rather, the 'Fourth' symbolised the city's only direct link with soldiers instantly recognisable as her own and, as such, was the epitome of Dundee's human contribution to the war effort. In the winter months of 1917-1918, Joseph Gray, himself a soldier in the 4th Black Watch and one of the journalists of the D.C. Thomson offices who would be known throughout the city as 'Fighter Writers' wrote as the First World War continued:

> ...it is the Fourth Black Watch that essentially personifies for us both the splendour and sorrow of our sacrifice. Individually we may follow the fortunes of other units, but in the Fourth the whole city finds glory in victory and grief in adversity.[6]

The largest numbers of the 4th Black Watch's recruits were drawn from the city's three historical institutions: the jute mills, jam factories and journalistic offices. In contemporary newspapers, 'Dundee's Own' is often used as a broad term not only referring to the 'Fourth', again illustrating that the citizens were not only interested in one battalion. The 'Fourth' served as an instantly recognisable symbol for Dundonians fighting everywhere; even when explicit reference to 'Dundee's Own' is made, an implicit recognition of Dundee's wider contribution is undoubtedly present.

Not only a city of jute and marmalade, Dundee was – and to a large extent still is – notable for journalism, mainly through the long-existing empire of D.C. Thomson & Co. Although John Leng & Co also dominated in the 19th century, from 1905 this company was increasingly owned and controlled by D.C. Thomson.[7] Collectively they were responsible for reporting the progress of the War both in terms of national news, as well as following local men on the various fronts of the War. For the Dundee newspapers, the 'Fourth' presented a unique and – as will be explored – a crucial means of maintaining a direct link between Dundee's citizens and her soldiers at home and abroad. Individual letters and presents were sent to individual families, but the newspapers represented a unique form of connection between citizen and soldier during the First World War under otherwise isolated circumstances. With its strong journalistic tradition, Dundee serves as an ideal subject for a study of the role of the provincial press during the Great War. It boasted two daily morning papers, the *Dundee Advertiser* and *The Courier and Argus*, as well as an incredibly popular weekly periodical, *The People's Journal.* Each of these papers varied significantly in tone, content and readership, and furthermore each showed a great deal of interest and dedicated much space to information regarding the progress of the War, in particular its local dimension traceable in the story of the 'Fourth'.

The role of the press in scholarship on the First World War is becoming increasingly important, bringing out a neglected human dimension of Britain's involvement in the conflict. Using Dundee as a relevant and indeed crucial case study for examining the role of the provincial press during the War, this book will concentrate on the newspaper reportage of Dundee's local Territorial Battalion, mostly through printed letters, poetry and featured articles. Alongside these sources, other first-hand accounts include William Linton Andrews's eloquent memoir *Haunting Years* (1930); a fascinating diary by a young gentleman called Alexander Thomson; an account of the 'Fourth' by Joseph Gray; the Commanding Officer Lieutenant-Colonel Harry Walker's field service book; and the poetry of Joseph Lee. Another resource is the extraordinary collection of letters of two Dundee brothers, Sidney and Harvey Steven, which serve as a case study at the end of the book. These stories, each in their own ways, encapsulate the tale of 'Dundee's Own' as one of both great pride and profound sorrow. Chapter One introduces a general overview of the role of the press in the First World War, indicating how it can contribute to knowledge and understanding of the war, in many ways challenging deep-rooted assumptions about soldiers' experiences. Chapter Two analyses the composition of the 'Fourth', evaluating how far it can be seen to characterise the city of Dundee, and considering the battalion as a cohesive network of mutually respectful men, often regardless of rank or background. Chapters Three to Five serve as a chronological account of the 4th Black Watch, beginning with the process of recruitment at the outbreak of War, through to what was perceived as their regrettable amalgamation with the 5th Black Watch in mid-1916.

The 'Fourth' provided the citizens of Dundee with a tenable link by which to follow the often isolating and confusing progress of the First World War, particularly through its newspapers. By claiming the relatively small collective of soldiers as 'Dundee's Own', Dundonians very clearly and deliberately claimed ownership over their symbol and expression of Dundee's wider First World War experience. Eric Linklater, a famous Scottish writer and Private in The Black Watch, noted the specialness of the 'Fourth' as an explicitly Dundonian battalion, expressing that its citizens 'mourned their losses with a special poignancy' as each casualty represented a loss directly for Dundee.[8] The 4th Battalion comprised around 1,000 men, all of whom were either existing territorial soldiers or new volunteers drawn from the city of Dundee itself, including all its major officers. It was a short-lived battalion, mobilised in the later months of 1914 and sent to the Western Front in spring 1915, and throughout that year it participated in a number of important battles. Most famously, the 'Fourth' played a role in the battle most closely associated with Dundee's memory of the First World War, the Battle of Loos, which one commentator has termed 'Dundee's Flodden'. As a result of its decimated ranks following this battle, the 'Fourth' was amalgamated with its Angus counterpart, the 5th Black Watch, ending the tale of 'Dundee's Own' just over a year after leaving Dundee from Dudhope Palace. Following the men of The Black Watch's 4th Battalion, from the battalion's mobilisation to its amalgamation, and using the words both of its citizens and its soldiers, this book is their story.

NOTES

[1] A. G. Wauchope, *History of the Black Watch in the Great War*, vol. II. (London: Naval & Military Press Reprint, 2002) (original pub. 1925), p. 3.

[2] *The People's Journal*, 16 May 1925.

[3] T. C. Smout, *A Century of the Scottish People* (London: Collins, 1986), p. 267.

[4] Wauchope, p. 3.

[5] *The People's Journal*, 27 February 1915.

[6] Joseph Gray, 'The 4th Black Watch in the Great War', *Dundee Advertiser*, 3 December 1917.

[7] Throughout the rest of the text, the name D.C. Thomson & Co will be used to describe the joint empires of Thomson and Leng.

[8] Eric & Andro Linklater, *The Black Watch* (London: Barrie & Jenkins Ltd., 1977), p. 142.

Chapter One
'Poison Gas Projected In Print'?
The First World War Press on Trial

'All that I have read in the papers...has been perfectly correct'.

Lieutenant Sidney Steven, 4th Battalion, The Black Watch

17 March 1915

Assessing the Bad Press of the Press since the First World War

The story of the provincial press during the First World War has been virtually untouched by historians. Two exceptions to this otherwise tenacious rule are Adrian Faber and Stephen Badsey, both of whom have recently published valuable research which places the press in its rightful place on the historical map of the Great War at long last.[1] Both of these historians, who have done much to fill a gaping void in the otherwise well-established historiography of the First World War experience in Britain, were perplexed by the desertion of the press, which ignited their ground-breaking research. This book intends to continue this work in a Scottish context, specifically in the news-centric city of Dundee. It will argue that local newspapers should – and viably can – be seen as crucial portals into understanding wartime public opinion. In a study of this length and nature, it would be an unrealistic goal to examine accurately the role of all Scotland's copious papers during the First World War. Catriona M.M. Macdonald's estimation that over 300 separate newspaper titles were in regular publication and circulation by the eve of war in 1914 both highlights the limited scope of this book and makes the case for further work to be undertaken.[2] Although the parameters of this study are limited, and a far broader and more comprehensive exploration of Scotland's wartime press wanting, this book will argue, as a case study reflecting broader issues, that the local press in Dundee is a legitimate and significant resource for researching the experience of the First World War in many ways.

An historical analysis of First World War provincial newspapers undoubtedly develops a fuller understanding of the attitudes and experiences of local citizens at home, and soldiers fighting abroad. By concentrating particularly on the local press, an altogether more human picture of the war emerges. Following the dramatic rise in popularity of newspapers throughout the Victorian era and into the Edwardian period at the beginning of the twentieth century, newspapers were the leading contemporary form of mass media available to the public. With the wide variety of newspapers that were readily available in Britain, it is hardly surprising that newspapers were undoubtedly the first frame of reference for the citizens of Scotland during the turbulent years between 1914 and 1918.[3] It has already been mentioned that Dundee provides an ideal focal point for this study. Dundee possessed one mainstream newspaper distributor, D.C. Thomson & Co (which also owned John Leng & Co), but this company was hugely influential throughout and far beyond the confines of the River Tay. Based in offices on Bank Street right in the city centre, D.C. Thomson was innovative, powerful, and commanded the attention of a wide and diverse readership, which it reached either daily or weekly through its principal newspapers and periodical: the *Courier and Argus*, the *Dundee Advertiser* and *The People's Journal*. The first of these, the *Courier and Argus*, was aimed explicitly at readers within the professional – especially business – classes of the city. Second, the *Dundee Advertiser* was more concerned with the daily happenings within the city, and possessed an entirely different, and altogether more accessible, tone compared to the *Courier*. Lastly, *The People's Journal* was a weekly periodical published every Saturday, which was immensely popular with the Scottish working people, not only within Dundee: its various editions enjoyed a wide circulation throughout Scotland.[4]

During the Victorian era, newspapers catered for a learned but still comparatively small section of Scotland's educated community, but by the end of the nineteenth century this paradigm had shifted: newspapers now aimed to facilitate all levels of society. *The People's Journal* in particular was a product sprung directly from Lord Northcliffe's late-Victorian innovation for newspapers 'to cater for the new generation of educated and literate working people'.[5] Northcliffe's national version of this ideal paper of the masses was the *The Daily Mail*, a world precedent of the first mass-circulation daily newspaper, and Dundee took inspiration from this new trend with the creation of the hugely successful weekly periodical *The People's Journal*. Thoroughly illustrated, containing more colloquial language and structured more creatively than the small-printed, regulated columns of Dundee's daily newspapers, the periodical's task was to summarise the week's events in Dundee, Britain, the world, and the war in a manner that the working people of the city could understand.

Despite the press's newfound imperative to inform the literate twentieth-century public through affordable newspapers containing accessible language and easily digestible articles, the prevailing perception towards the wartime press has remained wholly scathing. Just ten years after the close of war, before a widespread anti-war mindset prevailed, Arthur Ponsonby had only harsh words for the wartime press:

> Acting on behalf of their country, with issues at stake of such vast significance, they do not hesitate to lend themselves to a deliberate attempt to mislead their people and the world, and to endeavour to justify their attitude by resorting to the meanest tricks.[6]

Another historian, Philip Knightley, in *The First Casualty* (1975), a book dedicated to exposing the war correspondent as 'hero, propagandist, and myth maker' throughout history, ferociously attacked the First World War press. He asserted that 'more deliberate lies were told than in any other period of history', continuing vehemently that the entire British nation 'went into action to suppress the truth'.[7] Somewhat apologetically, Colin Lovelace observed that 'the mud has stuck' with regards to traditional judgements surrounding the wartime press.[8] The ferocity of these accounts suggests that, no matter how potentially valuable an analysis of newspapers published during the First World War might be, the biased perceptions and often incorrect assumptions about the role of the press are so firmly cemented in scholarly and public perception of the history of the war that such negative views are virtually impossible to undo. Further intensifying this unfortunate rejection of the press in the narrative of the Great War, it is clear that historians are unwilling to regard newspapers as viable resources for historical research because the press is 'burned beyond recognition by the acid of censorship and propaganda'.[9] In short, so long as the press is associated with the notorious Defence of the Realm Act (DORA) – with which it is inextricably linked – the voice of the press is to remain, somewhat ironically, suppressed.

Defence of the Realm?

The Defence of the Realm Act was put into action in the first few weeks of the First World War, and still possesses the ability to reduce any British newspaper house to a shudder. The memory of the Act remains as one of the most controversial government measures, alongside conscription and execution of deserting soldiers. The tenets of DORA, an act created to prevent communication with the enemy or the spread of false or confidential reports, were expanded and modified six times during the four years of the First World War. It granted the British government unprecedented power 'to issue regulations for securing the public safety and defence of the realm', and the ability to punish those who broke them.[10] So far as this concerned the press, in theory, any articles printed would need to be carefully monitored in case information about movements or planned conflicts were printed. Modern historiography concerning DORA concludes that it engendered a press of absolute oligarchy, a system of draconian censorship that smothered journalism outright until the Act was dissolved. Philip Knightley, continuing his tirade, outlines what motivated the newspapers' acquiescence with the censorship but, more importantly, what it sacrificed in the process:

> In Britain, under the Defence of the Realm Act, a system of censorship was created so severe that its legacy lingers today. The willingness of newspaper proprietors to accept this control and their co-operation in disseminating propaganda brought them the rewards of social rank and political power. But it also undermined public faith in the press.[11]

The famous historian Arthur Marwick described DORA as 'that cruel and capricious maiden who at the snap of her fingers could close down a newspaper', alluding to the absolute power possessed by the government under the veil of this legislation.[12] Under it, the Asquith government created a Press Bureau – nicknamed the 'Suppress Bureau' by journalists – which was wedged between the War Office and the Admiralty, as well as being attached to the Home Office.[13] Allowing only for carefully altered and distorting stories from the battlefield, DORA has been remembered as a tyrant that heavily prosecuted any publication that dared defy the legislation.[14] As a result, the press ultimately failed in its main purpose during the years of the First World War: to inform and to discuss.[15]

Although there were indeed cases where newspapers were prosecuted for dissenting from the Defence of the Realm Act, such as the briefly suppressed *The Globe* and *Labour Leader*, the Press Bureau, not being an independent department, could only recommend prosecutions of newspapers to the other departments it served. In many cases, the delay necessary for this procedure of prosecution regularly defeated the purpose, and so penalties were relatively rare or mild.[16] Therefore, despite regular prosecutions for DORA-dissenting newspapers being prevalent during the First World War, recent research has highlighted evidence which shows the Act did not have the level of authority over the press as previously assumed. Viewed as a largely ineffective operation, the *Dictionary of Official War-time Organizations* defined the Press Bureau's aims: 'to supervise, largely on voluntary basis, issue of news to and by press, and to prevent information of value from reaching the enemy'.[17] The use of the phrase 'voluntary basis' already undermines the urgency found in every mention of DORA, but historians dismissing the reliability of newspapers during DORA's reign rarely investigate the role of the Press Bureau itself. The leading defender of the press in wartime, Dr Stephen Badsey, states that the Press Bureau 'normally went no further than to issue editors with guidance on which subjects were to be avoided or treated with caution, and the draconian powers available to the government were only rarely used'.[18] Indeed, even relatively early on into the war years, the Press Bureau was regularly castigated, which provoked a response from the Home Secretary which was published in the *Dundee Advertiser* in October 1915:

> [As] if it was possible for one highly skilled individual to read the whole of the material submitted in a continuous stream night and day by every newspaper office and from correspondents in all parts of the world...That, however, is manifestly impracticable. Consequently the work has to be done by a large staff...who do their best to apply the general rules laid down to the matter submitted. It no doubt happens from time to time that the particular individual who is trying to apply these rules makes a slip. All that can be said on that head is that the Directors of the Press Bureau do their very best to reduce such mistakes to a minimum...[19]

The above description of the Press Bureau, the national body created especially for the strict censorship of the British press during the First World War, is presented sympathetically, which is perhaps surprising concerning mainstream attitudes of censorship through DORA. M.L. Sanders and Philip Taylor argued in their book *British Propaganda during the First World War* (1982) that the Press Bureau was largely unable to control the press, which remained determined and relatively free both to criticise and to interpret the news with relative freedom, in spite of the wartime restrictions.[20]

For all intents and purposes, the British press was simply far too powerful, and too vast, for any government legislation to control, never mind wholly repress.[21] The Home Secretary's letter in response to criticism of the Press Bureau is revealing in its defensiveness, and adds an altogether human, imperfect stance to counter the common dread of absolute power that connotations of DORA arouse in modern historians:

> It is doubtless an extremely convenient arrangement, when national necessity requires that a press censorship should be set up, to be provided with a whipping boy, particularly if he will stand a good deal of castigation without flinching.[22]

The above portrayal of the official British organ for press censorship as a helpless and submissive scapegoat is incredibly telling. Furthermore, Adrian Faber uncovered in his research a relatively unknown exchange of correspondence between Sir George Riddell, chairman of the Newspaper Proprietors' Association, and Sir Edward Cook, co-director of the Press Bureau, from 1915.[23] In response to Sir Riddell's bewilderment that the provincial press appeared to possess far more freedom than the national newspapers, Cook admitted defensively: 'we do not every day examine all the thousands of papers'.[24]

Such a revelation throws into question the legitimacy for a continued assault upon the wartime newspaper during the period 1914-1918. Further research addressing the role of the Press Bureau, its effectiveness and its processes of censorship is required, particularly concerning the provincial press. In comparison to the national press, such as daily British newspapers like *The Times* and *The Daily Mail*, and Scottish national dailies such as *The Scotsman* published in Edinburgh, the above discussion and evidence provides ample suggestion that newspapers in centres like Dundee enjoyed relatively little interference from government censorship. Due to its extensiveness, community boundaries and heavily working-class readership, the provincial press was in many cases viewed as 'politically unimportant'.[25] During the Great War, the lack of attention given to the local press meant that requests for items such as personal cameras in correspondence often slipped past the censor. Evidence of this lack of state intervention is clear to see in the published photographs in newspapers, and the letters and private photograph collections of soldiers such as Lieutenant Sidney Steven of the 4th Black Watch. These factors clearly suggest that local newspapers during the First World War were granted a greater degree of freedom than has been previously assumed. The little research that has been done on the newspapers of the First World War has been almost entirely focused on the national press, and it is time the attention shifted to the newspapers of cities such as Dundee as not only a valuable but a vital source of understanding wartime public opinion. Indeed, there is much evidence both in recent historiography and in the newspapers themselves that the information supplied is far from 'poison gas projected in print'.[26]

A Misunderstood Source of Study: The Value of the Great War Provincial Press

The sheer vastness of provincial newspapers afforded freedom to the press, but editors were entrusted to avoid revealing compromising details to the public. D.C. Thomson was proud in its self-censorship, viewing itself as a responsible and patriotic newspaper that would never have allowed the publication of anything that would defy Regulation 18: the supply of information useful to the enemy.[27] As shall be seen throughout this book, despite limitations imposed by DORA and the necessities of self-censorship, Dundee's citizens were generally well informed of the 4th Black Watch's whereabouts. Furthermore, managers of the Dundee press viewed the provision of regular, accurate information relating to the war as its duty, enhanced of course by motives to continue its impressive circulation and readership. Clearly, more research addressing the role of the Press Bureau and its levels of censorship is required, but even at this early stage the traditional ignorance of the wartime newspapers is wholly unjustified and requires urgent reconciling if an accurate and authentic understanding of the people's experience of the First World War is to be achieved by historical means. The prevailing perception of the wartime press, asserting that the lack of stories as a result of censorship caused newspapers to exaggerate and sensationalise events, is widely accepted and has remained relatively uncontested until recent years. Indeed, Dundee's own literary sociologist, Bruce Pandrich, has little but contempt for the Dundee wartime press as 'justifying' the losses of the 'Fourth' through euphemistic sensationalism.[28] In his MPhil thesis about Dundee's experience of the Battle of Loos – which he somewhat melodramatically terms 'Dundee's Flodden' – he argued that 'euphemism was used to tone down horror, to make the unacceptable acceptable and to sustain a myth which inspired men to fight for their lives in the most horrible conditions'.[29]

William Linton Andrews, a journalist and war volunteer, straddled the two worlds of the Dundee press and the 4th Battalion of The Black Watch. His account of the 'Fourth' in action is invaluable as he affords an insight simultaneously from the press' desire to boost morale during war, but as a man in a place to assess the accuracy of what the reports depict. In his memoir, Andrews states that 'our men would much have preferred to be described as suffering heroes up to their knees in blood' as opposed to having their life depicted in rosy colours.[30] Although this was at times a habit indulged in by *The People's Journal*, even that most fervently patriotic periodical adopted a solemn tone after the Battle of

Loos in September 1915, publishing material describing 'Dundee's dark hour' that will be discussed later in this book.[31]

Provincial newspapers have for too long been confined to local history collections in libraries and archives with only sparse, intermittent independent research being conducted by amateur and local historians. A far broader study of the newspapers, which have never constructively been analysed from an historical perspective in the context of the First World War, is required in order to explore Badsey's intriguing claim that '[journalists] were allowed considerable latitude in their writings, and the belief that they either lied outright or failed to describe the horrors of the Western Front is a myth'.[32] It is partly the purpose of this work to continue the revisionist work of historians such as Badsey who condone the reportage of the provincial wartime press. More specifically to the Dundee context, this book aims to emphasise that Pandrich's analysis of the Scottish city's experience is largely unfair and, judging by the available evidence, somewhat distorted. As will be discussed throughout this book, Dundee's newspapers did in fact publish many letters depicting the negative and horrific experiences of men in the 4th Black Watch, and that positive articles published were not necessarily examples of false or sensationalist reportage. This chapter has argued that the Scottish provincial press is an important and worthwhile source in understanding local public opinion during the First World War. Indeed, local newspapers have much to say about many issues currently being addressed by First World War historians: the use of propaganda in recruitment; class structure of men at the front; conscription; and officer-man relationships. It may be some time before this claim can realistically be accepted into the mainstream historical narrative of the First World War, and the path towards this acceptance necessitates the daunting task of tackling Scotland's hundreds of volumes of diverse newspapers.

Whilst this book cannot hope to achieve such aims alone, it ultimately aims to tell the story of the 4th Black Watch, and of Dundee's contribution to the First World War, through its local newspapers. Such inquiry and revisionism is particularly poignant as the centenary for the outbreak of the Great War looms. There is palpable evidence to suggest that there is far more truth in the pages of the provincial press than has been erstwhile accepted, or perhaps expected. The roots of exploration, finally, are planted.

NOTES

[1]   See both Adrian Faber, 'The Provincial Press During the First World War: A Case Study of the Wolverhampton *Express & Star* between January and March 1918', Unpublished MA Dissertation (University of Birmingham, 2006) and Stephen Badsey, 'Press, Propaganda and Public Perceptions' in Michael Howard (ed.), *A Part of History: Aspects of the British Experience of the First World War* (London & New York: Continuum, 2008).

[2]   Catriona M.M.Macdonald, 'Race, Riot and Representations of War' in Catriona M.M. Macdonald & E.W.McFarland, (eds.), *Scotland and the Great War* (East Lothian: Tuckerwell Press, 1999), p. 147.

[3]   Gerard J. DeGroot, *Blighty: British Society in the Era of the Great War* (New York: Addison Wesley Longman, 1996), p. 181.

[4]   Jonathan Rose, *The Intellectual Life of the British Working Classes* (New Haven & London: Yale University Press, 2001), p. 114. The *Courier* was a Thomson publication while the *Advertiser* and *People's Journal* were published by Leng. Thomson also published the *Evening News* and *Weekly News* and Leng the *Evening Telegraph*.

[5]   Philip M. Taylor, *Munitions of the Mind*, 3rd ed. (Manchester: Manchester University Press, 2003), p. 174.

[6]   Arthur Ponsonby, *Falsehood in War-Time* (U.S.A: Kessinger Publishing, 1928), p. 145.

[7]   Philip Knightley, *The First Casualty: The War Correspondent as Hero, Propagandist, and Myth Maker from the Crimea to Vietnam* (London: Harcourt Brace Jovanovich, 1975), p. 80.

[8]   Colin Lovelace,'British Press Censorship During the First World War', in G. Boyce, J. Curran & P. Wingate (eds.), *Newspaper History: From the 17th Century to the Present Day* (London: Constable, 1978), p. 307.

[9]   Faber, p. 4.

[10] Defence of the Realm Consolidation Act, 27 November 1914.

[11] Knightley, pp. 80-81.

[12] Arthur Marwick, *The Deluge*, 2nd ed. (London: Macmillan Press Ltd, 1991), p. 76.

[13] DeGroot, p. 182.

[14] Trevor Royle, *The Flowers of the Forest* (Edinburgh: Birlinn, 2006), p. 93.

[15] Marc Ferro, *The Great War* (London: Routledge Classics, 2002), p. 139.

[16] Lovelace, pp. 312-313.

17   N.B. Dearle, *Dictionary of Official War-time Organizations* (London: Humphrey Milford, 1928), p. 310.

18   S. Badsey, 'Press, Propaganda and Public Perceptions', pp. 28-9.

19   *Dundee Advertiser*, 12 October 1915

20   M. L. Sanders, & Philip M. Taylor, *British Propaganda during the First World War, 1914-18* (London: The Macmillan Press Ltd., 1982), p. 22.

21   Lovelace, p. 307.

22   *Dundee Advertiser*, 12 October 1915.

23   Faber, p. 6.

24   Ibid. p. 6.

25   S. Badsey, 'Haig and the Press', B. Bond & N. Cave, (eds.), *Haig: A Re-appraisal 80 Years On* (South Yorkshire: Pen & Sword Military, 1999), p. 180.

26   Gary Sheffield, 'Officer-Man Relations, Discipline and Morale in the British Army of the Great War', H. Cecil & P. Liddle, (eds.), *Facing Armageddon: The First World War Experienced* (London: Leo Cooper, 1996), p. 727.

27   Lovelace, p. 312.

28   Bruce F. J. Pandrich, 'Dundee's Flodden: a Sociological Study through the Written Word', University of Dundee, Unpublished M.Phil thesis, 1988, p. 28.

29   Ibid. p. 45.

30   W. L. Andrews, W.L., *Haunting Years* (London: Naval & Military Press Reprint, 2001) (original pub. 1930), p. 88.

31   *The People's Journal*, 19 February 1915.

32   S. Badsey, 'Press, Propaganda and Public Perceptions', p. 33.

Chapter Two
Citizens and Soldiers Too
Who Were the Men of the 'Fourth'?

When we read the magnificent story
Of all that our heroes achieve,
When proudly we think of their glory
And the honour their names should receive,
Then we long, with a thrill of elation,
To blazon their merits afar -
Till we find with intense irritation,
We are not even told who they are!

- Anon, 'An Appeal'
The Dundee Advertiser, 19 May 1915

In the final pages of notes in the personal field service diary of Lieutenant-Colonel Harry Walker (see Plate 12), the Commanding Officer of the 4th Battalion The Black Watch, a scrawl specifies that 30 officers and 860 other ranks had arrived at the rest camp near Le Havre in February 1915.[1] All drawn from the professional and working classes of Dundee, these men, Dundonian by birth or not, were now 'Dundee's Own'. As shall be seen throughout the following chapters, which depict the chronological story of the 'Fourth' during their time in France, relations amongst the men and officers were important to the men themselves, and to the people at home. It was picked up on by the newspapers of the city, which aimed to portray the battalion as a coherent unit of men and officers who were happy to work and live amongst each other. By all that can be derived from official and first-hand accounts, as well as reports in the newspapers and letters to families, this spirit of camaraderie was not difficult to discern, and certainly did not need to be forged. The strength of this solidarity is remarkable considering the vastly different circumstances from which many of the men derived. This chapter will concentrate on the social composition of the 4th Black Watch, identifying particular groups where possible, as well as general association and cohesion amongst the ranks. In particular, it is concerned with the representation of the officers in the battalion, as well as those soldiers who have left the modern reader their fascinating first-hand accounts, such as Sidney and Harvey Steven, Alexander Thomson, William Linton Andrews, Joseph Lee and Joseph Gray. First, however, the chapter will turn to the matter of officer-man relations, which is becoming an increasingly prominent theme in the study of the First World War.

When discussing officer-man relations relating to the British Army in the First World War, it is abundantly clear that generalisations are difficult and dangerous. Challenging the perceptions made popular in the 1960s by Liddell Hart and Alan Clark has proven an almost Herculean task for revisionist historians. Hart and Clark introduced the now famous 'lions led by donkeys' paradigm: the idea that the apparently inept generals and commanders at the very top of the military hierarchy – such as Sir John French, Field Marshal Douglas Haig and Lord Kitchener – cared nothing for the rank-and-file, and were happy to throw many thousands upon thousands of soldiers at the German machine guns.[2] It was just not as simple as that. Although this study is not primarily concerned with the wider narrative of the First World War, and the complicated revisionist debates cannot be entered into here, it is important to note that these officers have been judged largely on the wrong basis, by modern rather than contemporary traditions of masculinity and character. With particular reference to Douglas Haig, who was demonised throughout the mid-twentieth century as a callous, unfeeling butcher by multiple commentators, a competing revisionist historiography has emerged to create a more balanced account of the successes and failures of the administration of the British Army.[3] Gary Sheffield, for one, has done much to deconstruct the strength of the mainstream collective memory which perceives officers as incompetent, upper-class fools who dismissed the soldiers as mere cannon fodder. Sheffield argues that 'we must judge Haig by the standards of his own time, not a later one', going on to observe that generals and other high-ranking officers 'had friends or even sons fighting in the armies under their command'.[4] Furthermore, in response to allegations that men like Haig felt nothing on hearing of mass casualties, Sheffield notices that Haig was profoundly affected by the death of his chief of staff, Brigadier General 'Johnnie' Gough, VC. Sheffield continues:

> We must be careful to distinguish between 'callousness' and ruthless determination to succeed. While some generals have doubtless been psychopaths, most are normal human beings who have had to come to terms with the human cost of their decisions...Haig's apparent callousness was in reality part of the mental make up of every successful commander, 'the robustness' to withstand 'the shocks of war' to which Field Marshal Wavell referred in his celebrated lectures on generalship.[5]

Indeed, the reappraisal of officers in the First World War can be specifically applied to the experiences of the 4th Black Watch and their encounters with high-ranking officials. William Linton Andrews's memoir of his time on the Western Front is particularly illuminating in the rank-and-file soldiers' perceptions of high-ranking officers. For example, Major Wauchope, whose history of The Black Watch in the First World War indicates the greatest respect and gratitude towards soldiers, and in particular the Territorial troops, was in many ways a similar man to Haig in terms of staunch character and apparently emotionless attitude. Having to deal on a daily basis with reports of men's deaths, Andrews observes his technique at dealing with such news:

> A familiar voice, that of Major Wauchope, nephew of the famous general of the South African War, was [at Port Arthur] receiving reports. A runner would come up and say in a breathless, broad Scots voice: "Lieutenant So-and-so has been killed, sir, and second-lieutenant has been badly wounded, but we've got him to the first-aid post."
>
> Major Wauchope: "Very good."
>
> Another report: "Three officers of such-and-such a company have been killed. Captain So-and-so and Lieutenants So-and-so and So-and-so."

Major Wauchope: "Very good."

> I saw much of this officer later. He was a born fighter, a man of
> military genius. It thrilled me to hear his "Very good," calm and
> soldierly, concealing intense grief at the loss of brother officers.
> Useless to regret them then. One had to carry on, and he did
> with noble self-control.[6]

Responding to Wauchope's attitude, Andrews was far from disdainful
of such apparent dismissiveness, and instead respected his ability to
move on not only from the deaths of rank-and-file men but also those
of officers, with whom Wauchope was likely to be professionally, if not
personally, familiar. Andrews's perceptions of Wauchope related
directly to his professional capacity despite tragic circumstances. This
example confirms Sheffield's argument that the ordinary soldiers of the
First World War, rather than appreciating a commander who showed
great emotion and struggled with the news of unabating casualties,
would be more impressed with an emotionally restrained, professional
reaction. As will be seen with the 'Fourth' men's relationships with
officers, particularly the Commanding Officer Harry Walker, the first-
hand accounts and newspapers demonstrate a resounding and
enduring respect for his ability to remain dignified and staunch in the
face of casualties and adversity. These were, the men saw, the right
qualities of leadership, and did not interpret their professional attitude
as heartlessness. These different interpretations of the soldiers show the
experience of high-ranking officers and administrators dealing with the
death of officers and men for whom they were responsible in a starkly
different, and altogether more human, light.

Understanding the role of officers within individual regiments and
battalions has remained both complicated and contentious. This
section of the book is primarily concerned with the representations of
officers in the 'Fourth', as well as the battalion's encounters with some
of the most famous commanders of the British Army. However, this
study cannot speculate on the relations between officers and men other
than the 'Fourth'. For a wider discussion, the work of Gary Sheffield,
one of the foremost revisionist historians in the field of the First World
War, is revealing. He has found that informal relations on active service
between officers and the rank-and-file were a main feature of life in the
war, drawing attention to the great many letters from officers which

show 'devotion, even love, for their men', and are suggestive of a paternal role.[7] Those officers who showed poor leadership skills and showed no care towards their men or who did not 'behave in a gentlemanly fashion' would lose the respect of the troops who would not follow them, no matter how prestigious their commissions.[8] In his study of officer-man relations at a platoon or battalion level, Sheffield concludes that 'it is rare indeed to find a blanket condemnation of officers in the writings of other ranks', and that 'the generally excellent state of officer-man relations had important consequences for the morale of the army of 1914-18'.[9] In the 'Fourth', there were no identifiable coups or even major gripes relating to the officers. In fact, the findings with regard to the 4th Black Watch support the argument that relations amongst the officers and men were generally very good. These relations contributed to the high morale and the freedom felt among the troops to enjoy themselves, but respect for their officers would always limit the extent of this freedom. Indeed, rather than a relationship led mainly by the officers in control, it was a dynamic one in which the rank-and-file would respond and reciprocate. It was not a one-sided paradigm.

Before moving on to discuss the rapport between officers and the rank-and-file in the 'Fourth', it is first appropriate to provide some background relating to the officers of the battalion as conveyed by the Dundee newspapers, as well as further information where appropriate. In 1914, immediately after war was declared and mobilisation began, The People's Journal produced a series of articles entitled 'Citizen Soldiers' throughout autumn and winter of that year, each article depicting a brief biography of the officers involved in the 'Fourth'. These articles were in part to stimulate recruitment, but they also provided informative details about the men in charge of 'Dundee's Own' Battalion, in which the people of the city more generally were very interested. By ascribing to the title of the article the phrase 'Citizen Soldiers', the newspaper was clearly making a point; that although these men were officers, they too were Dundee men. The first in this series, on 8 August, perhaps unsurprisingly delineated the character of the battalion's Commanding Officer, Lieutenant-Colonel Harry Walker, a wealthy local businessman. Walker was a central figure both to the battalion and to the reportage in the Dundee newspapers, and described by William Linton Andrews as our 'beloved commander' who was 'in the judgement of Dundee and of his men, the finest type of civic soldier'.[10] The article on Walker in *The People's Journal* had the following to say of him:

> Colonel Harry is one of our captains of industry: he is also a leader in commerce, being President of the Dundee Chamber of Commerce; and he takes active interest in our beneficent institutions. Throughout his strenuous business career he has devoted special attention to national defence. In the Volunteer service he took a leading part as an officer...In every department of the service he was an earnest student and practical militarist, winning the golden opinions of Army and Volunteer chiefs and of his fellow officers and men.[11]

When the Territorial force was formed, Walker was second in command until ear-marked to succeed Colonel Howard Hill in 1910. Following that accession and prior to mobilisation, Walker 'has striven to rouse interest in the home defence movement' and has been 'indefatigable in his efforts to make his corps one of the very best'.[12] Walker's men clearly thought very highly of him, and those who commented on his nature and his relations with the men were overwhelmingly positive, despite his being a man of such high professional and military standing. According to Andrews, he led the battalion with a business-like level of precision, but also addressed the men more informally in giving them lectures on the importance of putting the battalion before oneself:

> We were always glad to have our Commanding Officer, Colonel Walker, at our billets, even though he came to tell us the old, old story, for he had a brisk, businesslike address and he made us feel that to run the battalion on strict military lines would be first-class business efficiency, as indeed it would. His lectures to us made a big difference.[13]

As shall be seen throughout this book, the officers played an important role in their letters to families that were published in the press, as well as more personal interviews. Despite being responsible for a thousand men, Walker also took the time to write to the relatives of the wounded, a task normally undertaken by the Lieutenant in charge of the casualty's particular unit. The following transcript is taken from a folded sheet of carbon paper found in the back of his field service diary:

France

22/3/15

Dear Mrs Gray,

I hope you have good news of your boy and that he is making a rapid and satisfactory recovery.

As I promised you I have had his valise and various odds and ends collected and send them down to Cox's French forwarding Agency Rue de Victor Hugo Boulogne. San. Mer.

If this does not come to you in the course of a week or so will you write to Messrs Cox & Co.

Banden Charing X. London.

We are again on the move but perhaps when you hear of your son's condition you will kindly send me a postcard saying how he is going on from time to time.

Yours sincerely,

H. Walker.[14]

Walker will appear repeatedly throughout this book, but it seems that the standard set by the Commanding Officer trickled down among the other officers, as there was a widespread respect found for the 'citizen soldiers' by their men.

Captain E. Leslie Boase, a Senior Captain of the 4th Black Watch, was particularly popular with the men, and described by *The People's Journal* as 'one of our citizen soldiers upon whom a full share of hard work has devolved'.[15] Since the hour of mobilisation, the paper enthused, he was so busy and fastidious in his work to organise the battalion that 'Territorials and civilians regard him as Commander-In-Chief at Dundee headquarters'. With a well respected father in the city, 'the Captain is held in high esteem by all Dundonians', and a Director of the Boase Spinning Company which, it was emphasised, was a company local to Dundee. Boase also had political interests prior to the war as he was called to stand as the Unionist candidate for Dundee. Finally, the paper stated: 'As a soldier, Captain Boase is on active military service, but his record as business man, politician, and citizen soldier shows that he is on active service all the time'.[16] There are many references in first-hand accounts of officers' kindness towards the men that they saw as beyond necessary. Boase receives the most individual appraisals of this nature. Alexander Thomson, who had little interaction with Boase as he was not in his company, describes the following with a tone close to awe: 'Captain Boase commissioned me to buy two pairs of boots for two men in the company whose footgear had become the worse of the hard usage they had been getting. He himself paid half!!'[17] For those in Boase's company, the reports were no different. As the officer in charge of Andrews's company, there are numerous allusions in his account of the war that are extremely complimentary to the officer: 'our leader, our inspirer, I might almost say our spiritual father, Captain Boase', which adds weight to the aforementioned hypothesis from Gary Sheffield that there were strong and almost paternal connections between many soldiers and their officers.[18] Perhaps the most telling account was published in the *Courier and Argus* shortly after the Battle of Neuve Chapelle, at which Boase was wounded:

> If the people of Dundee…want a hero they have one ready made in Captain Boase, who apparently knows not the meaning of the word fear. At Neuve Chapelle he astounded most of us by his indifference to danger – I do not mean foolhardiness, but his calm, cool demeanour and the keenness he displayed in safeguarding the men under his charge…Although suffering severely, for he was shot through the chest, all his thoughts were for the comfort of his men. No wonder we were ever ready to follow him anywhere he might lead, and it is men like him who display such dauntless courage who will bring the Allies ultimate victory.[19]

Such testaments, this book argues, were not examples of meaningless hero-worship or newspaper propaganda, but as can be determined from the first-hand accounts of men who served under these officers, were discerning and heartfelt accounts of men whom they respected because the officers in turn showed the men the utmost respect.

Major Emslie Tosh occupied the space for the 'Citizen Soldiers' piece on 22 August 1915, and was described as 'one of Dundee's most ardent citizen soldiers'.[20] A chartered accountant by trade, Tosh had undergone an illustrious volunteer service in South Africa as a Lieutenant, before being selected to command a draft for the first volunteer company attached to The Black Watch. In this role, 'he soon gave proof of his abilities as a skilful leader of soldiers'. After volunteering on several campaigns in Africa at the beginning of the century, Tosh was also keen to prove his skill in Scotland:

> On the formation of the Territorial Force he became an active officer, rendering invaluable service to the movement in this quarter of Scotland. As an officer he has the confidence and esteem of his fellow-officers and of his men, and as a busy chartered accountant in the city he has the confidence and esteem of civilians.[21]

Other notable officers were Captain Norman Crawford Walker, a solicitor before the war and close friend of Sidney Steven, whose testimony appears throughout this book. Professions of the soldiers were seen as important in the biographies of the 'Fourth' officers, illustrating in the case of Walker 'that close and successful attention to a professional career does not preclude the giving of active and very valuable service in home defence'.[22] With the history of Scotland's regiments close to his heart, as well as many of the other officers described in the service, it was stated that Walker was very keen on building the fighting force of the battalion to procure fresh laurels in France and Belgium.

Other prominent officers such as Harry Walker's Adjutant, Major Tarleton of the 1st Black Watch, as well as the Medical Officer for the Battalion, Major J.S.Y. Rogers, went on to have prominent roles both in the life of the battalion and in the pages of the newspapers. Rogers was particularly respected and features heavily in the accounts of the newspapers and soldiers, particularly Andrews's memoir and Sidney Steven's letters. Andrews had the following to say of him:

> [The Medical Officer] was Major J.S.Y. Rogers, a name I cannot mention without feeling again the leadership and love in his outstanding personality. He was a perfect example of devotion to duty. He seemed to have the priceless War gift of being able to do without sleep, and when casualties were heavy brought to his work a spirit of healing that made many forget their pain. He was a brisk, hearty, and merciful man, one we poor soldiers thanked god for.[23]

Rogers became one of the Dundee newspapers', and as far as can be ascertained, the soldiers', favourites. This is exemplified by a report in the diary of Private William Rae, who said of Rogers shortly before his own death from wounds on 19 May 1915: 'There is one person whom I think should be recognised for his work, and that is Major Rogers, for he attended to the wounded under such fire as I never had imagined in all my wildest dreams, soothing and comforting them with words and actions.'[24] By introducing the officers on which there is the most material, however, a more illuminating and personal picture of life at the Front emerges. It is no accident that *The People's Journal* published fortnightly biographies of the most noble and trustworthy leaders of the newly recruited and currently in-training 4th Black Watch. The purpose of these articles was to form an association, not necessarily between soldier and officer, but to reassure the citizens of Dundee that their sons, brothers and husbands were not in the hands of anonymous strangers but were in the safe hands of 'our citizen soldiers': friendly, responsible and upstanding members of Dundee society who would take care of their men. According to this, it was not only the officer-man relations that were somewhat paternal, but also the reassurance fostered in this sense by the newspapers. From the short analysis above, it is clear that the officers had a close, personal and often paternal relationship with the men they commanded in the 'Fourth'. Considering this, and Badsey and Sheffield's aforementioned works on officer-man relations, this multi-class camaraderie in the 'Fourth' is unlikely to be unusual. However, such a strong spirit of solidarity in the 'Fourth' made the tragedy that struck the men and especially officers on 25 September 1915 all the more profound.

As has been recognised already, the ranks of the 'Fourth' were filled with remarkable speed, and a great deal of this enthusiasm was due to the reputation attached to The Black Watch. It was also, however, largely down to the officers who led them. There was a sense among the men that, rather than living 'each for himself', the members of the 'Fourth' instead had become 'members of a brotherhood-in-arms'.[25] This notion of a brotherhood amongst the ranks of a battalion, particularly one drawn from the same centre, is not unusual to find in records of the First World War. The somewhat utilitarian sentiments of many men in the 4th Black Watch show the extent to which they were emotionally and physically invested in both the war effort and their own section of the fighting force. This perception of life as part of a 'brotherhood' is a common theme throughout the first-hand accounts, echoed in the letters of Sidney and Harvey Steven, the diaries of William Linton Andrews and Alexander Thomson, and particularly accounts of speeches given by Lieutenant-Colonel Harry Walker. Of Walker's lectures on 'the old, old story', Andrews in particular picked up on the emphasis of what it meant to be part of a battalion:

> We began to realize in a way we never did at home that on duty a soldier must subordinate everything to the honour of the battalion. Even if he were done some gross injustice he might serve faithfully under the man who had wronged him. The soldier was nothing; the battalion was everything. We men might die. The battalion would carry on. These were sobering and steadying thoughts, but not stimulating.

Andrews's response to Walker's 'sobering' words on how the men should reject notions of individuality to put the battalion first were listened to, and to a large extent accepted. As can be found in Andrews's account, however, this utilitarian mentality was not accepted wholeheartedly and without question, although this was not detrimental the men's respect for their commanding officer.

Joseph Gray perhaps provides the best summary of the different men who assembled in the drill hall in the first days of the war in early autumn 1914:

> Here, indeed, are all sorts and conditions of men. They are dressed in civilian clothes, and are obviously drawn from all classes – professional men, mill-hands, clerks, labourers, each class seems to have its representative. Here stands a typical "knut" of pre-war days…On his right hand stands a barber's assistant from Reform Street, on his left a calendar worker from Baxter's Mill. Here a budding banker, there a journalist from the "Tiser". Between these latter a short heavily-built casual labourer, with tobacco-stained teeth, expectorates frequently when free from the sergeant's eagle eye. The entirely new conditions of life, with its strict discipline different in every detail from those under which we had previously lived, made an

indelible impression, but above all was the subtle feeling, almost undefinable [sic] at the time, that we no longer lived each for himself. We had become members of a brotherhood-in-arms.[26]

Gray's assessment offers a colourful picture of volunteers keen to do their duty in the First World War as coming from an array of avenues and settings of Dundee. Derek Young observed that, during the recruitment process, the city's recruiting office was 'practically invaded by men of all classes offering their services'.[27] During the first days, however, the infant battalion did not seem quite as cohesive as they later became, according to Gray's account above. Andrews in particular was doubtful about his new situation, and particular about those with whom he was soon to be serving as a soldier. As mentioned previously, Andrews had wished to join the Regulars and was met with surprise and bitter disappointment to learn that he was in fact joining the Territorial battalion of Dundee. He did not feel like this for long. At first, however, he describes that he 'found many of my comrades strange', and that the feeling towards him was similar. There was clearly a sense of class separation in the Drill Hall, and there was an incident in which Andrews's expensive fishing boots were stolen. Andrews asked a sergeant about what he should do, and the reply came: 'Watch yourself, laddie [...] They'll steal the milk out of your tea in this mob' without further discussion.[28] At first, Andrews was clearly discontent in his surroundings before the rigorous training began, complaining about the dirt on his clothes and the 'hooligans' playing football whilst he tried to sleep. However, two things occurred to change his outlook.

First, a contingent, though not a clique, of men from the offices of D.C. Thomson, which included the poet Joseph Lee, and Andrews's friends Joseph Gray and Joseph Nicholson, joined the ranks of the battalion, who called themselves 'Writers and Fighters Too'.[29] The Dundee newspapers naturally attached a great deal of attention and affection to this group, which consisted of around a dozen members of the 'Fourth' who had enlisted from the newspaper offices. It is from these men that come the majority of letters published in the papers, the first-hand accounts left behind, and of course the poetry and sketches of Joseph Lee, which offer such a unique insight into the experiences of the soldiers. Not only was this small, close-knit collective followed avidly by *The People's Journal* and *Dundee Advertiser* – less so by *The Courier and Argus* – but these men also read their own and others' reports in the Dundee press when these were available to them at the Front. Although anonymous in the newspapers, the early movements of the Battalion can be followed in the letters sent home by Andrews and his comrade, Joseph Nicholson. The poetry and sketches of Joseph Lee also add a dynamic touch to the pages of the *Advertiser* and the *Journal*, as his *Ballads of Battle* – published in 1916 – represented brilliantly the different elements of trench life: grief, humour and, most explicitly, camaraderie.

Second, Andrews had complained of the delay in getting uniforms for the first week or two, which had arguably allowed the newly enlisted men to view their new occupation as something of a novelty, or even a holiday. Andrews observed wryly that 'you can't make a man a soldier without a uniform' and, indeed, once these were available and the real training began, different backgrounds faded away alongside class consciousness.[30] The men were now of the same battalion, and recognised, at last, that they were defending the same city. It became particularly clear to them through training, and especially when the troops reached France, that regardless of rank or background they were working together and formed a common bond. Acknowledging that although there were times when disagreements arose these were relatively few and minor, Andrews later commented on the cohesion of the battalion: 'we quarrelled less than men do in a business office'.[31] Furthermore, Andrews showed that he had drastically changed his views from the first days in the Drill Hall to the removal of the battalion to France by pointing out: 'There was never the faintest trace of class feeling. Men showed very little interest in what their comrades had been in peace time'.[32] This newfound identity in the 4th Black Watch meant that the soldiers, no matter what background, could remove themselves from their individual past and concentrate on their soldiering present as a member of a unit. Volunteers from the jute mills and jam factories of Dundee were bundled into the barracks with men from professions such as accountancy and banking. Despite the seeming disparity of lifestyles between these men during peacetime, the personal accounts of W.L. Andrews, the Steven brothers and Alexander Thomson coincide with newspaper reportage of a sense of 'brotherhood' in the ranks of the 4th Black Watch across all classes.

Eric Linklater, one of the most famous novelists of the Scottish twentieth-century literary renaissance and an officer with The Black Watch during the Great War, singled out the case of the 'Fourth' in particular, arguing that it was justly referred to as 'Dundee's Own' due to the diversity among its ranks: 'Neighbours in a street, and the men of a family, had joined its ranks as Territorials, so that now they mourned their losses with a special poignancy'.[33] The newspapers of the city attached particular meaning to this idea of all Dundee's occupations, ages and backgrounds in its battalion, which as suggested earlier was representative of Dundee's wider experience in the war. The newspapers, therefore, took up their role in uniting soldiers and civilians. In his work, Adrian Faber argues that this was also true of the provincial press in Wolverhampton later in the war, as he argued that 'the only divide between the two was distance [...] Community and localness united home and battlefield as one'.[34] Conversely, Bruce Pandrich argued that, rather than acting as a bond between soldier and civilian, the newspapers contributed to a 'widening gulf' between the two centres of war, as the newspapers were unable to do justice to 'the indescribable nature of [the soldiers'] experiences.[35] Although the latter point may have an element of truth, the Dundee newspapers regularly admitted their inability to report precisely the official movements of the 'Fourth', but as can be seen from their fastidious reportage, the newspapers attempted as best they could to produce as accurate a portrayal of the soldiers' experiences as possible. The result of this ambition has allowed a book of this nature to be written, since the newspapers of Dundee committed themselves to publishing numerous letters sent from the Front to Dundee, as well as expressing the views of Dundee citizens at home through poetry and letters to the editors. It is from the reportage of the newspapers that modern readers can know and appreciate the views of the soldiers, their families at home, and perceptions of themselves as brothers. If it were not for these reports, modern readers would and could not appreciate the respect held by soldiers for their officers and commanders, how they felt during their experiences and afterwards, and how they found the strength to report deaths of friends, colleagues and loved ones. Without such interpretations, the story of the First World War is detached and inhuman, similar in many ways to Alan Clark's definition of officers as apparently heartless 'donkeys'.

NOTES

1   Lieutenant-Colonel Harry Walker, Field Service Book, Black Watch Regimental Archive, MS 0296.

2   Alan Clark, *The Donkeys* (London, 1961).

3   See in particular Brian Bond and Nigel Cave, (eds) *Haig: A Reappraisal 70 Years On* (Barnsley: Pen & Sword Military, 1999) and its more recent revision *Haig: A Reappraisal 80 Years On* (Barnsley: Pen & Sword Military, 2009).

4   Gary Sheffield, *Forgotten Victory: The First World War, Myths and Realities* (London: Headline Review, 2002), p. 137.

5   Ibid. p. 138.

6   Andrews, *Haunting Years*, pp. 56-57

7   Gary Sheffield, 'Officer-Man Relations', p. 414.

8   Ibid., p. 419.

9   Ibid. pp. 420-421.

10 Andrews, *Haunting Years*, p. 159.

11 *The People's Journal*, 8 August 1914.

12 Ibid.

13 Andrews, *Haunting Years*, p. 96.

14 BWRA, Harry Walker Field Service Book.

15 *The People's Journal*, 19 September 1914.

16 Ibid.

17 Alexander Thomson, Diary, 13 March 1915, Black Watch Regimental Archive, MS. 0712.

18 Andrews, *Haunting Years*, p. 144.

19 *The Courier and Argus*, 20 May 1915

20 *The People's Journal*, 22 August 1914.

21 Ibid.

22 *The People's Journal*, 26 September 1914

23 Andrews, *Haunting Years*, p. 68.

24 *The Courier and Argus*, 27 May 1915.

25 *Dundee Advertiser*, 3 December 1917.

26 Ibid.

[27]   Derek Young, *Forgotten Scottish Voices from the Great War* (Gloucestershire: Tempus, 2005), p. 18.

[28]   Andrews, *Haunting Years*, p. 15.

[29]   Ibid. p. 20.

[30]   Ibid. p. 14.

[31]   Ibid. p. 87.

[32]   Ibid. pp. 87-88.

[33]   Linklater, *Black Watch*, p. 142.

[34]   Faber, p. 51.

[35]   Pandrich, p. 58.

Chapter Three
'A Flame of Valiancy'
Raising Dundee's Own Battalion

Wha'd bide at hame, callants, wha'd bide at hame?
To sit in idle comfort, or play the witless game?
Oor sires, when Honour beckoned, bore aye the battle's brunt;
Shall Scotsmen sell their birthricht? Nay! Let us to the front!

- Anonymous, 'Recruiting Song'
The Dundee Advertiser, 12 February 1915

'Your King and Country Needs You': Early Recruitment and the 4th Black Watch

As the spring and summer months of 1914 continued, the prospect of war loomed progressively until, on 4 August, Britain declared war on Germany. The origins and run-up to the outbreak of the First World War have been thoroughly documented by historians of the past century and need not be entered upon here. From the outset of war, the national and provincial newspapers of Scotland had a prominent role in rallying support, which, according to *The Scotsman* of 5 August 1914, was considerable from the start. However, at the beginning of August there were no British troops as yet stationed in continental Europe, and it would take two weeks before the first divisions of the British Expeditionary Force (BEF) set sail for France.[1] Field Marshal Horatio Herbert Kitchener (1860-1916), the Secretary of War, was widely considered the finest living soldier in Britain at the time, and his role in the recruitment process was crucial. Trevor Royle claimed:

> to the man in the street...Kitchener could do no wrong. His career had seen him move from victory to victory...and his very presence - his huge frame, his luxuriant moustache, the fixity of his gaze - had become the symbol of British pluck and resolve.[2]

Kitchener sought a solution to the problem that Britain's professional army was not big enough as it numbered only 247,432 men at the time: huge numbers of men would need to be enlisted to bring it up to strength. Consequently, on 8 August the instantly recognisable 'Your King and Country Needs You' propaganda poster was distributed widely throughout Britain, and the newspapers called for 100,000 volunteers aged between 19 and 30 who 'have the safety of our Empire at heart' to enlist for the British army. As well as the creation of his now-famous 'New Army Battalions', volunteers were called for to fill the ranks of the existing territorial battalions throughout the country, of which the 4th Black Watch was one.

Back in Dundee, *The People's Journal* quickly cemented its leading role in the recruitment process, proudly spreading the message of enlistment. One of its many headlines advocating the call to arms – 'Kitchener's Clarion Call to Scotland' – contained the following:

> At once the "People's Journal" set about sending the appeal of the War Secretary throughout the country. From John O'Groats to the Tweed, in the densely populated cities, in the remote glens and villages, in the sea-swept islands the call to arms was sounded by the "People's Journal".[3]

On the very day this 'clarion call' was sounded, *The People's Journal* boasted that the volunteers currently comprising the 4th Battalion of The Black Watch were 'Ready, aye ready', and 'fit for active service', in a successful attempt to draw young volunteers to enlist in the local Territorial Battalion for the City of Dundee.[4] That Dundee's own battalion was part of the 'legendary' Black Watch was an exciting prospect to the young men of Dundee eager to enlist.[5] In his history of The Black Watch, Eric Linklater intimated that the soldiers serving in that regiment over its 200 years of activity prior to the First World War had 'leapt again and again to a flame of valiancy' whenever its services were required, and its response to the recruitment drive in the autumn of 1914 was no exception.[6] Another historian of The Black Watch corroborates the regiment's reputation for duty and service when he describes the 'clamour to volunteer' for its various battalions at the outbreak of the First World War, which created an 'instant and massive' expansion of the famous regiment.[7] Those who volunteered in Dundee and were drafted into the 'Fourth' were keenly aware of the tradition they were joining, as expressed in the words of one journalist who volunteered: 'we meant to do our best for the honour of the Black Watch, the pride of Dundee. We felt that loving eyes at home were upon us'.[8]

These words are those of William Linton Andrews, one of the self-styled 'Fighter Writers' introduced in the previous chapter. Although there are several first-hand accounts written by men of the 'Fourth' available, Andrews's memoir *The Haunting Years* is unique as it is the only one that delineates the recruitment process. Andrews volunteered two days after war was declared in what he described as the 'swarming street outside the recruiting-office at Dundee'.[9] After fighting his way through the 'mob of old militiamen and unemployed' to reach the recruiting sergeant, he was asked if he was unemployed, to which Andrews replied that he in fact had 'a goodish job' as News Editor at the *Dundee Advertiser*. In response to this, he was apparently told, 'Then you make way for us lads wi'out jobs' and was hustled to the edge of the crowd forthwith:

> Funny (I thought to myself), I never knew it was so hard to become a soldier. I waited an hour or two. Still no good. I went back sorrowfully to my desk, and tried again the next day, and the next.[10]

Such an anecdote adds weight to the argument that it was not just propaganda and jingoism that stimulated recruitment, but that socio-economic reasons were also an important motivation for joining the army. Andrews was determined to join a Regular battalion, 'one that must be in the fighting line', and after a few days of persistence enlisted under the impression that he was, at the very least, a 'Kitchener man', if not a Regular. Andrews's assumption was soon proven to be a mistake, but prior to this discovery he signed articles for the *Dundee Advertiser* to assist with the recruiting process as 'By One of Kitchener's Hundred Thousand'.[11] Andrews attributed the *faux pas* to the 'unprecedented confusion of the recruiting-office', of which Andrews had the following description that affords a fascinating insight into the Dundee recruitment office:

> Men were ready to sign anything, and say anything. They gave false names, false addresses, false ages. They suppressed their

previous military service, or exaggerated it, just as seemed to promise them best. Recruits had to sign as fast as they could. They did not trouble to read their papers…'[12]

Such descriptions of commotion in the Nethergate recruiting office in Dundee, 'where smaller but no less enthusiastic crowds gathered' are indicative of the wider recruitment phenomenon in the early days of the war.[13]

Not surprisingly, London witnessed the largest numbers of volunteers, with a national report printed in *The Scotsman* on 8 August informing the public that 1,500 men had enlisted in the first three days of the war, and that more recruitment agencies were being set up throughout the capital to cope with the demand.[14] Yet the far smaller city of Dundee was drawing, proportionately, an impressive number of recruits at the beginning of the war. In *The People's Journal* of 15 August 1914, under the headline 'Dundee Rallies to the Flag', colourful anecdotes were printed to emphasise the success of the recruitment process:

> "Dundee has made a grand response," said a perspiring recruiting officer. "We are indebted to the 'People's Journal' for the patriotic action in rallying the men of Scotland."[15]

Elsewhere in the article, the reporter details a conversation overheard on the street nearby the recruiting office in the city:

> "Let's go now," I heard a young man say and, leading the way, he took three of his comrades with him. They are now in the Black Watch uniform.[16]

Reports such as the above, which were written to persuade like-minded young men who were unsure whether or not to enlist to take the opportunity in a moment of impulse, were somewhat typical of the jingoistic *The People's Journal*, which as described in Chapter One was a working-class newspaper prone to bouts of sensationalism. Although also a patriotic and staunchly British newspaper, the *Courier and Argus* was essentially a business paper targeted at the professional classes of Dundee, but an influential one that held the largest circulation 'north of the Forth'.[17] With its more sensible disposition, it was unusual to find sentiments such as those of Dundee's Recruiting Officer, Major Thomas

M. Cappon printed in the *Courier*:

> I would not be human if I failed to express my own pride and satisfaction as R.O. for the area, for I doubt if any other officer holding the same position could show a class of recruits more representative of the commercial life of the city and district...it is not possible to misjudge [the recruits'] spirit when one hears them take the oath of fidelity, and listens to their reasons voluntarily offered for not coming along at an earlier date.[18]

A large proportion of traditionalist historiography on the First World War has focused on the manipulation of young men to enlist in the army. Bruce Pandrich, for example, stated that 'the naïvety of those men who joined the 4th Battalion Black Watch and the sincerity of their emotions is not easy to understand'.[19] As seen in the previous chapter, the 'Fourth' comprised many men of different ages, many of whom had chosen to enter the war for different reasons, but, as far as evidence can show, were sure it was what they wanted to do. For example, the 36-year-old Joseph Lee, who would soon become the famous poet of the 4th Black Watch, who suffered from bronchial asthma, is unlikely to have received much peer pressure to enlist. Nevertheless, one day Lee walked into the Drill Hall on Bank Street – incidentally the same street where the D.C. Thomson offices were – and when asked his age told the recruitment officer to mind his own business and said: 'just give me my kilt'.[20] Throughout Dundee, the eagerness to volunteer was evident. This enthusiasm is exemplified by the fact that the first unit of the 4th Black Watch – referred to as the 1/4th Black Watch as its first contingent – was brought up to strength, with the 350 men necessary to comprise the battalion attested within only a fortnight.[21] Immediately after the ranks of the first contingent were filled, the recruitment office began to take volunteers for the 2/4th Black Watch, which was also filled with men – still drawn entirely from Dundee – by October 1914.[22] The ranks of the 'Fourth' were not only filled with a speed that was remarkable for Dundee's size, but, as seen in the previous chapter, with a diversity that truly justified Linklater's and Wauchope's definitions of Dundee as 'a city at war'.

'A Natural Keenness to serve in France': The First Days of the 'Fourth'

From late August 1914 until February 1915, the young Territorial

Battalion, the 4th Black Watch, first occupied itself with a fortnight of training in Dundee's Drill Hall. Thereafter, the recruits were stationed at billets around Dundee on guard duty, mainly at the Tay Bridge and by Broughty Castle. William Linton Andrews remembered the first days of duty as 'happy days; lazy days' which he spent with his friends on the hillside overlooking the River Tay, on strict instructions from an officer:

> An officer had marched us to the hillside, and then said: "You can lie down and go to sleep. Any man who wakes the rest by snoring will be shot at dawn. Get back to the billets by 4.15, but not before. Fall out![23]

The artist Joseph Gray also remembered the relatively carefree early days of training prior to leaving for France. Each day, Gray described that 'each sweating recruit was convinced that at last perfection had been attained', before receiving a lecture from their officers pointing out their faults. Gray and Andrews both reminisced of the camaraderie experienced in the first days at the barracks, of which Gray stated: 'I don't think any of my comrades will ever forget those early days in Bell Street'.[24] Andrews clearly enjoyed the experience, detailing that 'it was just like being back at school', and the 'smiling August and September days' full of ease', but that they were simultaneously eager to learn: 'we picked up the rudiments of the job with some enthusiasm'.[25] Something that is clear in the accounts available of the men of the 'Fourth' during these days is their eagerness, and often their impatience, to leave for the Front. Wauchope's official history of The Black Watch during the First World War focused particularly on the 4th Black Watch's 'natural keenness to serve in France', pointing out that 'officers and men hoped eagerly for a more active sphere than the peaceful links of Buddon or the Tay Bridge, with its monotonous round of guard duties'.[26] However, as September 1914 drew to a close, the 4th Black Watch was still a far way from leaving the British Isles for the Western Front.

Although the 'Fourth' would not see battle until early 1915, the young battalion came face-to-face with a loss amongst their ranks far earlier than anticipated. On 24 September 1914, Private David Barnett, a 21-year-old Private of 'C Company', was killed whilst on sentry duty. Stationed in Wormit at the Fife end of the Tay Railway Bridge, Barnett was struck on the temple by a golf ball whilst two women were engaged in a competition a fair distance away, and he died the following day on 25 September: precisely one year before the Battle of Loos at which the ranks of the 'Fourth' would be depleted beyond recognition.[27] There appears to be no reaction to this incident in the accounts of William Linton Andrews or Joseph Gray, which may be largely explained as the 'Fourth' was at this time split into two, with Barnett's 'C Company' stationed in Wormit under Major Tosh whilst Andrews's, Gray's and Lee's 'G Company' was mostly billeted in Dundee as far as can be determined by the expressions in both memoirs. There was also little reaction to this tragic event in the newspapers: indeed, from the perspectives both of the press and the troops, the war was at this time looked upon as 'a gigantic merry-making'.[28] Considering the context of the war at this time, with the recent Retreat at Mons and Battle of the Marne, it may seem deliberately deceptive of the newspapers, and unnecessarily naïve of the soldiers, to have maintained such a carefree outlook. However, Andrews remembered that 'even what we had heard of the hardships of the Retreat from Mons, sometimes from the lips of wounded men, did not chasten our spirits. We envied those indomitable fighters their place in history'.[29] Further, when it is considered that Dundee's citizens had little widespread experience of wartime loss at this stage this is not so surprising, and perhaps even understandable. The 'excited and careless spirit' of the Dundee newspapers quickly adopted a more respectful and at times solemn tone when it reported the experiences of its own tangible human investment in the Western Front when the 'Fourth' left for France. But in those early months, as Andrews admitted retrospectively: 'It had not yet occurred to us that War was an exceedingly dangerous occupation'.[30]

As 1914 drew to a close and the first full year of the First World War began, an increasing sense of restlessness grew among the ranks of the 'Fourth'. In November, part of the battalion was billeted to Broughty Castle, on the outskirts of Broughty Ferry by Dundee, for guard duty around that part of the River Tay. In reaction to such a move, Joseph Gray complained: '[w]e didn't want to come to Broughty. We felt we had been cheated somehow. Coast defence, indeed! Why were we not at France?'[31] Enviously, the men of the 'Fourth' read accounts in the D.C. Thomson newspapers of their Angus counterparts, the 5th Black

Watch, who left for France in late 1914. To make matters even more frustrating for the men, the first contingent of the 'Fourth' took over the guards and duties that the 5th Black Watch had been responsible for before its departure, and so their 'monotonous round' continued.[32] In his memoir, William Linton Andrews directly addresses the reader in this part of his account:

> "But when are we going to get to the Front?" the impatient reader will be asking. Yes, my friends. It is just what we were asking all through those months.[33]

The general consensus among the ranks of the 'Fourth' was one of anxious anticipation, and the Dundee newspapers, particularly *The People's Journal*, were keen to emphasise the eagerness of their troops. In an article entitled 'Ready for Service' as early as 19 December, the newspaper informed the citizens:

> The men, who have been quartered in the city or suburbs since the commencement of the war, are now beginning to grumble about the routine work which they are daily called upon to do, and orders for their departure, in their opinion, cannot come too soon.[34]

This apparently endless banality, however, was not to last.

On 23 February, 1915, a young private called Alexander Thomson wrote of that morning: 'We rose as usual, little thinking this was to be our last morning in Broughty Ferry, and turned out sleepily for first parade'.[35] As confirmed by Joseph Gray's account, and those in the Dundee newspapers, rumours had recently been spreading that the Battalion was to move abroad, but there were some, as Thomson alludes to, who 'were beginning to fear that we were to be left in Scotland till the end of the war'.[36] However, the long-awaited order had finally arrived, and the 'Fourth' were instructed to prepare for movement to France on active service that very day. The accounts of William Linton Andrews, Joseph Gray and Alexander Thomson afford astounding and diverse historical perspectives of the reaction from three separate soldiers in the 'Fourth' which are invaluable in understanding the perceptions and views of the time. In order to illustrate the views of the 'Fourth', three excerpts, one from each account, are provided below. The first, from Andrews's *Haunting Years*, is the most understated:

> We were off to France, a whole proud battalion. Off to France!
> We were bright-eyed with excitement: our hearts danced for
> joy.[37]

Andrews's account emphasises a group of men not only ready or resigned to fighting in France, fighting which had already commenced and they had been reading about avidly, but a group of men who were desperate to get there. Joseph Gray's account on hearing the same news matches Andrews's remarkably:

> Men flung their bonnets in the air and cheered themselves
> hoarse. One enthusiastic spirit relieved his feelings by doing
> 'cart-wheels' on the floor, while another with fixed bayonet
> prodded his well-filled kit-bag, which for the moment
> presumably represented the Kaiser, until that ill-treated,
> unoffending article, protesting, burst open. All were jubilant,
> irrepressible. France! The trenches! The GREAT ADVENTURE![38]

Alex Thomson also made reference to the great enthusiasm felt by his fellow soldiers, but his account of the hours before leaving Dundee is altogether more personal. Private – later Captain – Thomson, the son of a well-off family with a share in the Verdant Works, was desperate to see his family before he departed for France that Tuesday. Scheduled to leave at around six o'clock in the evening, Thomson asked Lieutenant Gladstone if he could make a quick detour, and was told: 'I could go where I liked so long as I was back before five-forty-five'.[39] And so, Thomson and his friends sped off in his car to Carnoustie, where he had fifteen minutes to say his goodbyes to his mother and sister before returning to the parade ground at Dudhope Palace.

'A Wonderful Expression of a City's Feeling': The 'Fourth' Leave Dundee

'The 4th Are Off To ——' was the headline in *The People's Journal*'s account of the 4th Battalion's departure from Dundee on the evening of 23 February, 1915. At the time, it was not certain that the 'Fourth' would even be heading to France, but as the newspapers and first-hand accounts show, most assumed this would be the case. In addition to the personal accounts available as an insight into the thoughts of the men of the 'Fourth', local newspapers provide a more public report of the dramatic events. With the troops to parade at Dudhope Palace, the reports of the daily newspapers, the *Dundee Advertiser* and *The Courier and Argus* on the following day are understandably rushed. On 24 February *The Courier and Argus* reported under the headline 'Off To Serve King and Country' that 'the 4th Black Watch were not allowed to take their departure in comparative silence'.[40] *The People's Journal* – which appeared every Saturday – had several days to prepare its report of the proceedings. Consequently, the most thorough and comprehensive coverage of the 4th Black Watch's departure is indubitably in *The Courier*, including numerous photographs and eye witness accounts.

The People's Journal, of the three Dundee newspapers being covered in this study, had the highest reputation for jingoistic sensationalism. Indeed, its report of the battalion's departure published on the 27 February boasted that the display showed 'the true Imperialism of Britain'.[41] However, there is more emphasis on the 'relative silence' with which the soldiers were watched as they slowly departed in separate contingents. Similarly, the *Courier* described an impressive turnout of citizens who had gathered along the parade: 'behind the collective boisterousness of a crowd there were many touching illustrations of the sadness of farewell'.[42] Assembled at Dudhope Palace from the late afternoon until around 6.30pm, the Brigade Major Captain K. M. Caird addressed the men:

> Men of the 4th Royal Highlanders, the chance has come for you to show in the field those high qualities which have always made the 4th Black Watch a Territorial battalion with which it is an honour to be associated. Men, you belong to a great Regiment, one whose battalions of the line have gathered glory and reaped fame in every quarter of the globe. You have a great tradition to sustain, and I trust that when you proceed on active service, to whichever destination you may be sent, you will remember that tradition and do your best to garner fresh laurels for The Black Watch. I myself have every confidence that you will do nothing to tarnish the fair name of the Regiment. I think, indeed, you may be trusted to conduct yourselves in the way you should do as a Battalion of Scotia's premier Highland regiment - the 42nd Highlanders.

Thereafter, the 4th Black Watch departed Dudhope Palace in three contingents, the sight of which *The People's Journal* described as 'inexpressibly inspiring', and Major-General Wauchope termed 'a wonderful expression of a city's feeling'.[43] The departure of the 'well set-up, gritty battalion' was accompanied with cheers throughout the Tuesday evening, but a feature that was conspicuous by its absence was the sound of bagpipes. Although the first and second contingents left from Dundee's Caledonian Station at 5.20pm and 6.25pm respectively on specially arranged trains, the lack of pipes did not seem to dampen any spirits:

> A lusty voice struck up the chorus 'Are we down-hearted' and the volume of sound carried away on the breeze as the inevitable negative was given in answer showed that in soundness of lungs the battalion had nothing to fear.[44]

By the time the third and final contingent was prepared to leave from the Tay Bridge Station (See Plate 2), the pipe band of the 6th Black Watch had arrived from Crieff. 'Hielan' Laddie' and 'Happy we've been a' thegither' were played to a crowd that the usually business-like *Courier* described as 'immense'.[45] This batch of soldiers were led by the Commanding Officer, Lieutenant-Colonel Harry Walker himself, and the *Courier* dropped its largely commercial tone to describe the scene as this final contingent of 'Dundee's Own' moved off to France:

> The troops were in great fettle, and amid the lusty cheers, the skirl of the pipes, and the clanging of the Old Steeple bells the third detachment of the 4th Black Watch left Dundee at 8.20pm for "somewhere in France".[46]

William Linton Andrews reminisced on the scenes: 'our march to the station and the scenes there were of an excitement never to be known in peace-time. The streets were crowded all the way, for this was a city going to war'.[47] Alex Thomson stated that 'the enthusiasm on this occasion was great and we had indeed a royal send off', and Joseph Gray echoes the others with his description: '[a] thousand hands were outstretched to grasp ours, a myriad of voices shouted their wellwishes and farewells'.[48] There is a definite unity between the descriptions of soldiers and newspapers, with the general consensus that both city and battalion were in huge celebration and excitement at the prospect of the 4th Black Watch moving off to fight in France. Far from being wholly jingoistic, there can also be found mention of tears, sadness of farewell and prayers said for the soldiers by their families, but the over-arching memories of the 'Fourth's' soldiers and the reactions of the city's newspapers were that it was a fundamentally joyful affair. Nevertheless, Bruce Pandrich described the send-off parades for the 4th Black Watch as 'very poignant, ironic and disturbing' when their later experiences in France are considered. However, the three first-hand accounts used in this study were all written towards the end or well after war had ended. The fact that the soldiers recounting them do not recall the leaving parades with foreboding or a sense of irony suggests that, for those who experienced the event, did not feel they were 'ironic' or 'disturbing'. Pandrich is accurate, though, in describing the scenes on 23 February as poignant, of which there can be no dispute.

The newspapers reporting the send-off for the 4th Black Watch made it abundantly clear that 'Dundee's Own' battalion was already doing the city proud. The celebrations in the streets of Dundee on 23 February 1915, which Joseph Gray described as having virtually emptied the jute mills and journalist offices for the day, further justify the characterisation of Dundee as 'a city at war'. The newspapers' protectiveness of the 'Fourth' continued throughout its endeavours in France, and advocated a feeling of 'spiritual oneness' with the people of the city who could be connected with their soldiers across the English Channel. The local newspapers made this pride so clear in their keen reportage on every action of the 'Fourth' that Andrews stated confidently: 'Dundee was proud of us. There was no question of that. Other units were perhaps not so fortunate, but we were a city's own, Dundee's very own, and her first thoughts every day were for us'.[49] It can already be derived, even before the 4th Black Watch reached France, that the historical value of an understanding of the First World War using comparisons of local newspapers and first-hand accounts of soldiers is illuminating. Not only do the newspapers present public opinion effectively, the intriguing first-hand accounts of the soldiers with the 'Fourth' work in tandem to create a truly human picture of Dundee's Great War experience. This can, to a large extent, allow for an interpretation of the First World War that moves confidently away from the deeply imbedded 'lions led by donkeys' doctrine. On reading newspaper accounts, and especially first-hand diaries and memoirs, it is strikingly obvious that, for many soldiers, this was simply not the case.

In his 1930s memoir of his experience with the 4th Black Watch, William Linton Andrews tackled historians who, like Pandrich, insisted on portraying the soldiers of the Great War as helpless victims. In order to understand what these men actually thought and experienced, there must be more emphasis on expressions of the time. Allowing soldiers to speak in their own words can, as illustrated below, provide a strikingly different perspective:

> [t]here is a school of war-writing that derides those simple and honest emotions of ours, makes a mock of our eagerness to serve and our readiness to do our duty, and sees us only as poor, wretched animals, caught and tormented in a gigantic cage of steel and flame. It was not so in February, 1915.[50]

It is, after all, the historian's burden not to judge, but to understand.

NOTES

1. Royle, *Flowers of the Forest*, p. 28

2. Ibid. 28

3. *The People's Journal*, 15 August 1914.

4. *The People's Journal*, 8 August 1914.

5. Bob Burrows, *Fighter Writer: The Eventful Life of Sergeant Joe Lee, Scotland's Forgotten War Poet* (Derby: Breedon Books, 2004), p. 64

6. Linklater, *The Black Watch*, p. 18

7. John Parker, *Black Watch: The Inside Story of the Oldest Highland Regiment in the British Army* (London: Headline Book Publishing, 2005), p. 173

8. Andrews, *Haunting Years*, p. 46.

9. Ibid. p. 11.

10. Ibid. p. 11.

11. Ibid. p. 13.

12. Ibid. p. 13.

13. Derek Young, *Forgotten Scottish Voices*, p. 18.

14. *The Scotsman*, 8 August 1914.

15. *The People's Journal*, 15 August 1914.

[16] Ibid.

[17] *The Courier and Argus*, 4 August 1914.

[18] *The Courier and Argus*, 11 January 1915.

[19] Pandrich, 'Dundee's Flodden', p. 21.

[20] Burrows, *Fighter Writer*, p. 64

[21] A. G. Wauchope, *History of the Black Watch*, p. 4.

[22] Ibid. p. 4.

[23] Andrews, *Haunting Years*, p. 20.

[24] Gray, *Dundee Advertiser*, 3 December 1917.

[25] Andrews, *Haunting Years*, p. 21.

[26] Wauchope, p. 4.

[27] *The Scotsman*, 26 September 1914.

[28] Andrews, *Haunting Years*, p. 24.

[29] Ibid., p. 30.

[30] Andrews, *Haunting Years*, p. 24.

[31] Gray, *Dundee Advertiser*, 4 December 1917.

[32] Wauchope, p. 4.

[33] Andrews, *Haunting Years*, p. 28.

[34] *The People's Journal*, 19 December 1914.

[35] Diary of Alex Thomson, 23 February 1915.

[36] Ibid.

[37] Andrews, *Haunting Years*, p. 29.

[38] Gray, *Dundee Advertiser*, 4 December 1917.

[39] Diary of Alex Thomson, 23 February 1915.

[40] *Courier and Argus*, 24 February 1915.

[41] *The People's Journal*, 27 February 1915.

[42] *The Courier and Argus*, 24 February 1915.

[43] Wauchope, p. 5.

[44] *The People's Journal*, 27 February 1915.

[45] Andrews, *Haunting Years*, p. 31.

[46] *The Courier and Argus*, 24 February 1915.

[47] Andrews, *Haunting Years*, p. 31.

[48] Diary of Alex Thomson, 23 February 1915; Gray, *Dundee Advertiser*, 5 December 1917.

[49] Andrews, *Haunting Years*, p. 182.

[50] Ibid. p. 30.

Chapter Four
'Forward the Fourth!'
First Action at Neuve Chapelle and Aubers Ridge

A message frae the hameland,
A greeting to ye a',
Brave soldiers of our own Black Watch,
The gallant Forty Twa.

- J. R. Russell, 'To the Black Watch at the Front'
The Dundee Advertiser, 26 January 1915

Arriving in France

During the 4th Black Watch's overnight journey to Southampton on 23 February 1915, Alexander Thomson complained that nothing of note took place. He and his friends occupied themselves by trying their best to obtain at every stop whatever goods they could.[1] On arrival in Southampton, the 'Fourth' found that there was to be some delay before leaving on their ship, the S.S. *Rosetti*, during which lull the men were served bully beef and biscuits. Late in the evening the order was to move onto the *Rosetti*, the sleeping quarters of which were described as 'truly horrible' and a 'cattle pen' by Thomson and Andrews respectively, whilst Gray's presentation of the ship was altogether more graphic:

> The prospect was unpleasing. The vessel appeared to have been recently used for the transport of horses, for around the hold stood primitive stables, which advertised their presence in no uncertain manner by a most unpleasant odour…There was no shelter from the rain, no protection from the cold wind, as the covering had been removed, leaving the hold open to the sky. "Ah well," said one, "it'll be fine practice for the trenches."[2]

Also on board the *Rosetti* was a draft of 300 men of the Scots Guards, which served as proof to Joseph Gray that they were bound for France, 'that Promised Land'.[3] According to Andrews, the 'Fourth' men diffidently saw the Scots Guardsmen as 'magnificent in physique' and the 'very gods of war'.[4] On the evening of 25 February, the *Rosetti* finally embarked on its journey into the mine-infested waters of the English Channel, escorted by two destroyers. What had just two evenings before been anticipated with widespread excitement and eagerness was transformed into a night of misery aboard the ship.

The next morning, the troops were more than thankful when they disembarked at Le Havre on the sunny morning of 26 February. This was the first time that Alex Thomson had seen the entire battalion, transport machine gun section and all, at once, and in describing their formation prior to setting off Thomson proudly recalled that 'we really presented an imposing sight'.[5] After breakfast, the 'Fourth' were on the move, 'marching with skirling pipes and swinging kilts' on their way to their first destination.[6] Joseph Gray described the first march of the 'Fourth' in France in romantic terms:

> The canal twisted and wound its way ahead through the country, so that we of 'D' Company who marched in the rear could see the whole of the battalion as the men swung steadily forward. It was an inspiring sight, for the 1000 men covered a great stretch of road…The line of men ahead seemed endless, and…the sight was indeed thrilling.[7]

According to the separate accounts of William Linton Andrews and Joseph Gray, on passing a school during their march, the headmaster called for the children to sing 'God Save the King' in English to the troops. Thereafter, the troops progressed by train to Lillers, which was about twelve miles behind the Armentières-La Bassée sector of the British front. From there, the 4th Black Watch moved even closer to the firing line – around ten miles – as they stopped for a few nights at the rest camp of Calonne, where the soldiers slept in a barn and were allowed to wander around the little village, practise their French, watch aeroplanes and write letters, all with the muffled sound of gunfire in the distance. Thomson reminisced fondly of the sheepskin coats the soldiers were provided with during cold weather: 'It was very funny to see us all running about in the dark with the white jackets on, everyone shouting "Baa, baa".[8] Although there are very limited newspaper sources that document this stage of the journey, the first-hand accounts of the soldiers all suggest that the 'Fourth' were settling in well to their new life abroad.

On 4 March, the order was received that the 'Fourth' should pack up and get ready to move immediately. Alex Thomson recalled that 'everyone had his own idea as to where we were going'; naturally the trenches were on the minds of many.[9] In fact, the men were billeted that night at Richebourg-St Vaast, a shell-torn hamlet behind the village of Neuve Chapelle: around three miles from the front line (see Plate 3).[10] After a long march, the battalion was greeted with the following information:

> On arriving in the village we were given the cheery information that the place was shelled twice daily and from the look of things I was quite prepared to believe this. The church had been severely handled and a portion of the spire had been shot clean away.[11]

That evening, the men were instructed to sleep in their boots and be ready to move at a moment's notice, alerting the troops to the first hint of their turn for action. However, no such order was issued that evening and the following day both Thomson and Andrews give accounts of watching 'shell after shell plumping into the church tower' in the village, the men's first experience of being under enemy fire.[12] Indeed, whilst at their billets at Richebourg, Andrews detailed that during the day, the shelling was exciting for the soldiers to watch. However, when evening fell, and the troops were required to collect wood for the cooks, or on other working parties, enemy fire became an altogether more daunting experience. As Alex Thomson put it, in something of an understatement, 'we did not altogether like it'.

On 5 March, some companies of the 4th Black Watch were chosen to enter the trenches, where they were billeted in quarters with part of the 2nd Black Watch, with whom stories of Dundee were swapped. The following day, the 'Fourth' lost its first man. Corporal Ralph Dick, an 18-year-old apprentice accountant, was shot in the head by a stray bullet whilst in charge of a piquet at an advanced post during training duties in No Man's Land.[13] This was the first piece of tangible news –

since locations and activities could not be published in the newspapers for the sake of protecting the war effort – that tested the informative role of the Dundee newspapers. The reports describing the incident in *The People's Journal* and the *Courier* both printed a letter sent to Corporal Dick's parents by Captain E. Leslie Boase. Boase explained that 'I visited him and the others there late last night and he was well and cheery then', and Dick had told the officer that 'he did not feel in the least bit frightened' and 'seemed just in his place'.[14] Bruce Pandrich analyses the first death in the battalion with particular attention to Captain Boase's letter, which in his view 'uses euphemisms…to portray Dick's last hours as honourable and courageous although he was in fact killed by a stray bullet'.[15] From the details of the letter detailed above, however, there is no identifiable use of euphemism. Since Corporal Dick was entrusted to be in charge of an advanced listening post between the lines, surely acknowledging the soldier's courage and willing is far from unreasonable, but respectful.

By early March 1915, the newspapers of Dundee were accustomed to incorporating the actions of the 4th Black Watch into their various pages as far as possible. Amongst advertisements, recruitment notices and updates on the jute industry, war news was at the forefront of the Dundee press nearly every day. On the page immediately subsequent to the official war news – usually page six in *The Courier and Argus,* page eight in *The People's Journal* – the Great War was set into context with the 4th Battalion's movements in France. When officers' letters began to arrive with details of casualties and, when available, troop movements, D.C. Thomson saw a way to present a personal and interesting account of the war through the eyes of the 4th Black Watch. Pandrich argued, somewhat hyperbolically, that such letters from officers depicting casualties that were often printed in Dundee's newspapers always adhered to an elaborate code, adopting 'practical skill in the explanation of…death'.[16] These apparent letters of 'self-inflicted deception', which created 'misunderstanding' and encouraged 'myths of glory' among readers of the Dundee newspapers, are seen by Pandrich, essentially, as lies.[17] Indubitably, Captain Boase's letter and the newspapers of Dundee presented Corporal Dick's death in a manner that simultaneously reported the facts, but also aimed to maintain morale at home. However, given the newspapers' role as

Plate 1: 'On The Eve Of Departure': image depicting the inspection by General McKerrell before the 4th's departure. Captain Couper and Lieutenant-Colonel Harry Walker can be seen walking directly behind the General. (Courtesy of D.C. Thomson & Co Ltd).

Plate 2: A contingent of the 4th Black Watch departing Dundee from Tay Bridge Station, February 1915 (Courtesy of D.C. Thomson & Co Ltd).

Plate 3: Richebourg-St Vaast, where the Battalion spent some time in spring 1915. Photographed by Sidney Steven on 16 May 1915. (Courtesy of The Black Watch Regimental Archive, MS 5795).

Plate 4: Captain Air and Lieutenant Sturrock in 'Pioneer Trench', 1 July 1915. (Courtesy of The Black Watch Regimental Archive, MS 5795).

Plate 5: Lieutenants Shariff, Law and Captain Walker in a 'Jack Johnson' shell hole, dated 5 June 1915. (Courtesy of The Black Watch Regimental Archive, MS 5795).

Plate 6: The men in the trenches at Rue du Bois: Captain McIntyre, Major Muir and Captain Cooper are featured. (Courtesy of The Black Watch Regimental Archive, MS 5795).

Plate 7: Officers Cunningham, McIntyre, Smith, Tosh, Sturrock.
(Courtesy of The Black Watch Regimental Archive, MS 5795).

Plate 8: No Man's Land, taken on Sidney Steven's secret camera. He apologised for the fuzziness of the photograph, as he had simply stuck the camera above the parapet in order to take the shot. (Courtesy of The Black Watch Regimental Archive, MS 5795).

Plate 9 and 10: Two images of 'B' Company of the 4th Battalion in the trenches, summer 1915. (Courtesy of The Black Watch Regimental Archive, MS 5795).

Plate 11: Joseph Gray's painting of the 4th Black Watch, entitled 'After Neuve Chapelle (10 March 1915)', painted in 1921. (Courtesy of Dundee Art Galleries & Museums, with copyright permission from The Black Watch Museum).

Plate 12: Lieutenant-Colonel Harry Walker, commanding officer of the 4th Black Watch, mortally wounded at the Battle of Loos, 25 September 1915.
(Reproduced from *A History of the Black Watch in the Great War*, vol. II by A.G. Wauchope).

Plate 13: Self-portrait of Lieutenant Sidney Steven shortly before the Battle of Loos took place, during which he was killed. (Courtesy of The Black Watch Regimental Archive, MS 5795).

bridging the gap between soldiers and citizens, this is surely understandable, and is hardly overdone. The facts in the regimental diary match those of the newspapers. In his assessment of the Wolverhampton press later in the war, Adrian Faber briefly commented on the reporting of casualties in his dissertation, observing that 'there was a delicate line between telling the real story and not appearing disrespectful to the fighting men'.[18]

In Dundee, receiving a first-hand account from Captain Boase, a man who was one of the last to speak to the young corporal, allowed for a personal perspective on his death to be printed in the papers rather than simply a dry report of the incident. The information surrounding Ralph Dick's death in the newspapers was provided with minimum bravado and appears to be relatively understated. The *Courier and Argus* reported that Corporal Dick had told Captain Boase that 'he did not feel a bit frightened, as he rather expected to'.[19] This quotation hardly backs up Pandrich's contentions of sensationalist journalism depicting a fearless and stoic warrior. Rather, the newspaper report alludes to the death of a dutiful, brave and altogether human, young man. Cross-referencing the reports of Dick's death with the first-hand accounts of Thomson and Andrews suggests that the Dundee press could be relied upon to publish truthful, if not too explicit, accounts of tragedy occurring on the Western Front during the early stages of the conflict. Whether the papers continued to do so is open to debate, and the further issues regarding press reporting of casualties in the 4th Battalion – such as through the medium of soldiers' letters – will be discussed further below.

Reporting the Battle of Neuve Chapelle

The 4th Black Watch was attached to the Bareilly Brigade in the Meerut Division of the Indian Army Corps; each Brigade of the Indian Corps consisted of one British and three Indian battalions.[20] The Indian battalions comprising the Brigade were the 2/8th Gurkhas, 41st Dogras and 58th Rifles, which had already experienced a large amount of fighting since late-1914, with more to come. However, without such thoughts bothering them at present, the men of the 'Fourth' were delighted to discover that their Brigade also consisted of their Regular counterparts: the 2nd Black Watch. With many Dundee men also serving with the Regular battalions of The Black Watch, there were various meetings of familiar faces between the 2nd and 4th Battalions. The soldiers of the 'Fourth' greatly respected the men of the 2nd Black Watch, from whom they learned many things, but many found living alongside the Indian battalions a strange experience to begin with.

On the evening of 6 March, the same day Corporal Dick was killed, the rest of the battalion trudged from their billets in Richebourg-St Vaast to their station at Windy Corner, directly facing the village of Neuve Chapelle. Once they arrived at the front line, the tasks which occupied their first days in the trenches included sentry duty, constructing dug-outs and lengthening trenches. The men were given practical advice by the regular soldiers of the 2nd Black Watch, as described by Alex Thomson:

> Alistair and I found ourselves with two of the regulars and at once set to work to make friends. I felt that the situation was indeed a peculiar one. We had never thought much of soldiers or their ways yet here we were, hanging on the words of these two and listening with attention to all their remarks...Of course we were full of questions. How far away were the Germans? Three hundred yards! Gee!!! What like a place was this trench? How long had they been there? How long would [we] be in? And so on.[21]

Whilst soldiers like Alex Thomson were busy learning about trench life from the regulars, the 4th Battalion was now stationed with the rest of the Meerut Division for the first time. Letters reaching Dundee from the men of the 'Fourth' were stopped prior to the Battle of Neuve Chapelle, and no official information was printed in the papers prior to the fight. However, on 6 March, *The Courier and Argus* could specifically state that 'the roar of the big guns is now sounding in the ears of the 4th'.[22] Indeed, the accounts of both Andrews and Thomson show awareness of an imminent battle. The first fight in which the 'Fourth' would play a role took place on 10 March 1915, just over a fortnight after 'Dundee's Own' had arrived in France. So far, the men of the battalion had proved themselves competent in training exercises and billets, and the newspapers back in Dundee were detailing the progress of the 4th Battalion as accurately as possible. However, the first real test, not only of the 4th Black Watch but also of the Dundee press, was to present itself in the Battle of Neuve Chapelle.

On the morning of 10 March, the whole Battalion – except D Company, which was already in the trenches – faced the village of Neuve Chapelle at Windy Corner. Neuve Chapelle had changed hands several times that autumn, and had been held by the Germans since November 1914. By 7am, 500 British guns had opened fire on the German positions, during which the 'Fourth' lay in wait under bad cover, and sustained some injuries when the Germans counter-attacked. During the counter-attack, Joseph Nicholson reportedly turned to Andrews and exclaimed 'They're shelling our fellows!'.[23] At eleven o'clock Lieutenant-Colonel Harry Walker gave the order to move into battle, and the 'Fourth' joined in their first fighting of the War. William Linton Andrews recalled the experience in his usual eloquent manner:

> We were going into the biggest battle that had ever been fought, the battle that was to end the War, the battle that would outshine Trafalgar and Waterloo. We had to be there. We were proud to be there.[24]

If Andrews's ambitions were running slightly high at this moment, it serves to exemplify the enthusiasm with which the 'Fourth' went into battle (See Plate 11).

The Dundee newspapers were quick to report the actions of the 4th Black Watch in its debut appearance on the front line on 10 March, which was 'the first real British offensive' of the First World War.[25] According to the history of the Indian Corps in France, the 'Fourth' carried out its assigned objectives 'with great dash and determination'.[26] Soon after the battle, news of casualties suffered in the battalion slowly began to trickle into the pages of the Dundee newspapers, mainly in the form of letters from men of the 'Fourth' themselves. Sergeant Thomas Bowman, for instance, wrote to *The Courier and Argus*, describing that he feared 'some 25 of his comrades in the 4th Battalion' featured on the casualty list.[27] However, a letter from an officer sent to his father, which was printed in *The People's Journal*, placed the casualty estimate at 140.[28] Sometimes all the newspapers could do was admit that the information simply was not available; *The Courier and Argus* detailed in one report that '[u]ntil the official lists are published the exact number of casualties sustained by the battalion will probably not be known'.[29] At times, the information supplied in letters varied dramatically, particularly when a ban was placed on letters being sent from the Western Front to avoid positions being given away. There were therefore shifts between times when a great deal of information could be gleaned by Dundonians from the newspapers and times when next to no information was provided. Despite this, the people of Dundee recognised that at least some connection with the 4th Battalion's experience could be made through the soldiers' letters. As expressed in letters from citizens to the Dundee newspapers, and to their sons and brothers on the front, the citizens of Dundee were also thankful for this source of information that otherwise would simply not have been available to such a wide audience.

With little official information of the battle's progression being provided by the British authorities until well into March, the people of Dundee were still able to learn what 'Dundee's Own' had come through from letters published in the local newspapers. By mid-March, letters to the casualty's next-of-kin began to be published in the newspapers, usually written by the officer who led the injured or killed soldier's company. This was the case with Lance-Corporal John Loftus, a joiner, whose death was depicted in a letter from Captain N.C. Walker as 'instantaneous, being caused by the bursting of a shrapnel shell'.[30] Letters written to the casualty's family were relatively simplistic recollections of the soldier's death, generally reassuring the bereaved that death was quick, and that the soldier would be sorely missed in his company. Although the reports of casualties were rarely graphic, such thorough reportage would not have been as consistently possible in a national newspaper. As well as having to deal with far larger readerships, and also more closely monitored than the provincial press, newspapers like *The Scotsman* mainly reported individual casualties in a more impersonal format: 'Corporal John Knox wounded in the face, and Private John Cochrane'.[31] Reports of casualties in the national newspapers were often abbreviated versions of those appearing in the local press from the area of the soldier's residence, and naturally did not contain the same detail. Although national newspapers stated the necessary facts, there is no local level of sympathy, no addresses, occupations, photographs or family details of casualties, as found in the Dundee newspapers.

Personal interviews, particularly those given by officers, were popular in the Dundee newspapers. *The People's Journal* published an interview with Captain Moon of the 4th Battalion, which was conducted whilst he was on furlough in early April 1915. Captain Moon said that the newspaper accounts of the action at Neuve Chapelle 'were quite accurate, and gave an excellent idea of what happened on the eventful three days of March'.[32] When asked about the casualties of the 4th, Captain Moon stated, 'I fancy from 60 to 70 would cover them'.[33] This early estimate was relatively accurate, as the Battalion War Diary shows the final 4th Battalion casualty figures for Neuve Chapelle at around 80.[34] Only a month after the battle, newspaper readers of Dundee had a relatively good idea of the first substantial dent made in ranks of the 'Fourth'. The Dundee newspapers also had the endorsement of the soldiers. Lieutenant Sidney Steven, for example, stated in a letter home on 17 March 1915 that 'all that I have read in the papers about the attack has been perfectly correct'.[35]

It would appear that the Dundee newspapers had found an effective means to gain information about the 'Fourth' without upsetting the official organ of newspaper censorship, the Press Bureau. The Dundee press was quick to report on the dead and wounded of the 4th Battalion, and their speedy, thorough reporting was almost entirely due to the publication of letters from the front. Although the information in letters could occasionally be dubious, by cross-referencing both condolence letters and personal correspondence it was possible for the D.C. Thomson offices to identify soldiers who were killed or wounded with relative confidence before they were reported officially by the War Office. The newspapers had the difficult task of reporting casualties as truthfully as possible without causing the morale of the Dundee populace to slip. This was particularly pertinent during the recruitment drive for a third unit of the 4th Battalion being built up at the time. Nevertheless, despite these factors, it would appear that Dundee citizens were relatively well informed about the 4th Battalion's progress in its first offensive, even before official documentation was published.

The Battle of Aubers Ridge

During the spring of 1915, the daily newspapers of Dundee published dozens of letters from the front, and, as the official information from the

War Office was supplied, the letters proved themselves a legitimate source for intelligence regarding casualties. Captain Couper reported the death of labourer Private James Davie, shot in the head by a chance bullet while cleaning his rifle, in a letter to the unfortunate private's widow. He explained that 'it was a series of unlucky events that [Davie] was hit at all'.[36] Nevertheless, the officer's letter assured Mrs Davie that her husband 'died a soldier's death, the death we all want to die when our time comes – to go out quickly while doing our duty'.[37] The people of Dundee appeared to be under no illusions that casualties only occurred during battles, and they recognised that a 'soldier's death' was not only to be had when charging the enemy. The letters sent by officers from the Front about casualties also exemplified the attachments between officers and the rank-and-file, discussed in the second chapter of this book. For example, Lieutenant Sidney Steven wrote in his own letter of being affected by his platoon sergeant, MacDonald, having died overnight after joking 'in his usual cheer fashion' that he had never slept on a stretcher but was going to sleep on one that night 'just to try them out'. Steven is very brief about it, stating that 'we found him on it in the morning, dead' and that 'it was an awful blow to me and I did not feel right all day. He was one of the best of fellows, no words are good enough in his praise'. Steven rushed to organise MacDonald's funeral himself, at which the whole platoon marched into Vielle Chapelle to bury him, covered in the Union Jack and 'carried to the grave by his brother and his particular friends in the Battalion'. The pipes played 'The Flowers of the Forest' and followed by the platoon took his body to the cemetery, where the chaplain offered a short prayer and Sidney reveals that 'then we laid poor MacDonald in his grave'. He continues: '[t]he pipers played "Lochaber no more" and platoon fixed bayonets and presented arms. Afterwards we all marched back, a very sorrowful party'.[38]

Despite the steady punctuation of sparse casualties throughout the spring of 1915, by the beginning of May the Dundee newspapers were beginning to adopt an altogether more optimistic tone when reporting on the 4th Battalion. The casualty reports of Neuve Chapelle had finally subsided, and the newspapers now began to incorporate not only casualty, but personal accounts, from soldiers of the 'Fourth'. One typical letter appeared in *The People's Journal* detailing the 4th

Battalion listening to a German soldier singing to his comrades: 'The song touched us all. "I hope they don't pip that beggar," said one of us'.[39] The people of Dundee were also kept up to date with the movements of 'Dundee's Own' as far as possible, being informed when they were in trenches and when they were in rest camps. Official news was also proudly reported, such as on 10 April, when the 4th Battalion was congratulated during a 'great inspection'[40] by Sir John French, who stated, 'I cannot find words to express my admiration for the courage, the self-denial and the splendid fighting spirit of the Territorials in this war'.[41] The first honours awarded to the 4th Battalion on 29 April 1915 were given to Lieutenant Sidney Steven, who received a Military Cross, and to Sergeants Thomas Bowman and John Macdonald, who each received a Distinguished Conduct Medal, which was proudly reported in the Dundee press.[42] The first reserve draft of the 4th Battalion also arrived in France to join the original battalion, building up the already damaged ranks of the original unit. During the spring of 1915, Dundee's citizens generally had a fair idea where the 4th Battalion was, when they were there, and what they were doing, despite limitations of what the papers could safely print. The month of April appeared to be relatively quiet for the 'Fourth', but this reprieve from battle was not to last. From the end of April onwards, these personal reports stopped suddenly, and it became increasingly clear that the men of the 'Fourth' were once again readying for battle.

On 8 May, the 'Fourth' once again received their orders to move up behind the line at Aubers Ridge near Festubert, where the Germans occupied an advantageous position over the British in the trenches below the hillside. The battle commenced with an ineffective bombardment and failed advance by the Allied troops, before 'A Company' of the 4th Battalion attacked at 3.00pm with devastating consequences for its ranks.[43] Their offensive ended in failure, and the active company of the 'Fourth' suffered severe casualties. Lieutenant Sidney Steven wrote in a letter that 'men were being knocked out, right and left...I can't describe it. It was too terrible. No one can have any conception of what it is like unless they have been through it'.[44] Whilst the men of 'D Company' were being 'thrown away', Andrews explained that a regular soldier compared Aubers Ridge to Magersfontein – that great shadow in the annals of The Black Watch –

as they waited in the trenches during the offensive.[45] A week or so later, when letters were reaching Dundee once again, the newspapers began to publish letters sent from the Front. *The People's Journal* reported on 22 May that Aubers Ridge was 'a terrible battle', and a letter from Corporal John McDonald, published in the *Courier and Argus* on 18 May, depicted the violent scenes:

> I thought Neuve Chapelle was bad, but last Sunday was worse, and I do not want to see anything like it again. You saw nothing but men blown up [i]n the air, men with arms off, some with legs off, and some being burned to cinders. It was awful.[46]

Aubers Ridge precipitated a definite and sudden change of mood in the pages of the newspapers to an altogether darker tone, which would not relent until well into the summer months. The citizens of Dundee were used to frequent news of 'Dundee's Own', but were deprived of information for some time as accounts of what had happened at Aubers Ridge did not reach the newspapers until around 20 May. When news was again available, the letters and reports published in the newspapers defy the traditional view that newspapers either lied or omitted the truth in order to keep morale high and the people placated. As with Neuve Chapelle, letters from men writing home about their experiences were often the source of first-hand information regarding 4th Battalion casualties in May 1915. Private John Keith, for example, wrote to his wife regarding the death of Joseph Smith, a millworker, describing the moments of his comrade's death: 'His last words were, "Jesus, Mary, and Joseph, help me," and tears came from our eyes as he breathed his last'.[47] Casualty reportage following the Battle of Aubers Ridge was received surprisingly quickly and adds more weight to the claim that letters sent from the Front could be a reliable source of information. One letter suggested that '[casualties] number somewhere about 160 at the least…30 or thereby being killed' as early as 25 May, long before the official casualty list was received in dispatches.[48] The accuracy of this early estimate is impressive: the casualties of Aubers Ridge in the Battalion's War Diary amounted to 30 killed and 120 wounded on 9 May.[49] This huge loss of men from the 4th Battalion makes it hardly surprising that the Dundee newspapers, alongside the 4th Battalion, for a time lost their 'jauntiness'.[50] A letter from a Non-Commissioned Officer published in the *Courier* further defies

Pandrich's view of the press presenting euphemisms instead of facts, as it described the men of the 'Fourth' as 'a war-worn, weary and blood-stained battalion'.[51]

That the tone of the Dundee press changed considerably to a more solemn key after Aubers Ridge does not mean to say that tales of heroism were not also published. Lieutenant Weinberg was the first officer of the 4th Battalion to be killed, and his 'gallant' death in *The People's Journal* was portrayed as he stood atop the parapet leading his men onwards, shouting: 'Come on boys; we will give the beggars socks!' before being 'riddled' with bullets from machine-gun fire.[52] Another letter described Private James Black as bravely saying to a stretcher-bearer, 'Never mind me. Keep [the bandages] for some other body. I am gone', before dying a few minutes later.[53] These letters, which depicted the men of the 4th Black Watch as valiant and noble in battle, shared the same newspaper columns as letters delineating scenes of 'hell upon earth'.[54] There were moving tales of Private William Mitchell having to break to his sister the death of her husband – also in the 'Fourth' – which was published in the *Courier and Argus* under the headline 'A Brother's Mournful Task':

> How am I going to tell you what happened? James has been killed in action. He died a hero's death...James was one of the first to go, and as soon he was on the point of getting over a German bullet laid him low. It was horrible the shell and rifle fire that was raging around us. It is impossible to describe it on paper. The Germans had a good many machine guns trained on us, and they gave it us very hot. It was hell let loose upon earth...We have, I reckon about 200 casualties – the biggest we have yet had. Jim has done his duty, and died a noble death.[55]

That the newspapers reported such a range of vastly different experiences of the 4th Black Watch's experiences is not surprising. On the contrary, it suggests that the readership of Dundee's newspapers had access to diverse and first-hand reportage of the war, reflecting the contradictory emotions and experiences of Dundee's soldiers.

Gradually the spirits of the Dundee newspaper reports once again lifted, seemingly alongside those of the 'cheery, brave, excellent fellows' of the 4th Battalion.[56] A letter from Colonel Harry Walker to the powerful newspaper proprietor D.C. Thomson states, '[t]he spirit of the men is excellent, and the health of the battalion good'.[57] A sports event with the 2nd, 4th and 5th Battalions of The Black Watch was described in the papers as 'a great success', and Alex Thomson felt it brought 'the three battalions into closer touch than they had yet been'.[58] The newspapers, however, alongside the more experienced and altogether more serious men of the 4th Black Watch, matured in tone. Alongside the reports of fun events, camaraderie and mutual respect among all ranks of the battalion – and the city – had of course been affected, and continued to be affected, by the constant presence of loss. Although the 'Fourth' experienced no fighting during the summer months, 'a continual drain of casualties' continued throughout 1915.[59] The 4th Battalion War Diary shows that these were mostly in ones or twos, and mostly incurred by enemy snipers during working parties or trench-digging. Andrews, who retrospectively describes the emotional maturity of the Battalion beautifully throughout his memoir, described these steady casualties as 'never...in great numbers, but all the time bleeding away our battalion'.[60] One such casualty was a prominent 'Fighter-Writer', Joseph Nicholson, who was killed by a sniper in July, thus being 'cut down at the beginning of a career full of promise'.[61] A close friend of Nicholson was Andrews, who solemnly echoed words from a speech made after the Battle of Neuve Chapelle by Colonel Harry Walker: 'The men died: the battalion goes on'.[62]

NOTES

[1]   Diary of Alex Thomson, 24 February 1915.

[2]   Gray, *The Dundee Advertiser*, 5 December 1917.

[3]   Ibid.

[4]   Andrews, *Haunting Years*, p. 31

[5]   Diary of Alex Thomson, 26 February 1915.

[6]   Andrews, p. 32

[7]   *Dundee Advertiser*, 7 December 1917.

[8]   Thomson, 27 February 1915.

[9]   Diary of Alex Thomson, 1-4 March 1915.

[10]   Wauchope, p. 6.

[11]   Diary of Alex Thomson, 1-4 March 1915.

[12]   Andrews, *Haunting Years*, p. 33.

[13]   Ibid. p. 7.

[14]   *The Courier and Argus*, 11 March 1915; *The People's Journal*, 13 March 1915.

[15]   Pandrich, p. 32.

[16]   Ibid. p. 32.

[17]   Ibid.

[18]   Faber, p. 23.

[19]   *The Courier and Argus*, 11 March 1915.

[20]   Wauchope, p. 6.

[21]   Thomson, 6 March 1915.

[22]   *The Courier & Argus*, 6 March 1915.

[23]   Andrews, *Haunting Years*, p. 49.

[24]   Ibid. p. 46.

[25]   Ian F. W. Beckett, *The First World War: 1914-1918* (Essex: Pearson Education Limited, 2001), p. 166.

[26]   J. W. B. Merewether & Frederick Smith, *The Indian Corps in France*, 2nd ed. (London: John Murray, 1919), p. 260.

[27]   *The Courier and Argus*, 18 March 1915.

[28]   *The People's Journal*, 27 March 1915.

[29]   *The Courier and Argus*, 23 March 1915.

[30]   Ibid. 22 March 1915.

[31]   *The Scotsman*, 24 March 1915.

[32]   *The People's Journal*, 10 April 1915.

[33]   Ibid.

[34]   4th Black Watch Battalion War Diary, Appendix No. 3: Casualties, March 1915, Black Watch Regimental Archives MS 0441.

[35]   Lieutenant Sidney Steven, Letter of 17 March 1915, Private Collection. I am grateful to Mr William Longair for his copy of these.

[36]   *The Courier and Argus*, 7 May 1915.

[37]   Ibid.

[38]   Sidney Steven Letters, 17 March 1915.

[39]   *The People's Journal*, 10 April 1915.

[40]   Diary of Alex Thomson, 10 April 1915.

[41]   Wauchope, pp. 10-11.

[42]   Ibid. p. 11.

[43] Ibid. p. 12.

[44] Sidney Steven Letters, 12 May 1915. See Chapter 6 for a more thorough account of the offensive at Auber's Ridge from Sidney's perspective.

[45] Andrews, *Haunting Years*, p. 125; Diary of Alex Thomson, 9 May 1915.

[46] *The People's Journal*, 22 May 1915; The Courier and Argus, 18 May 1915.

[47] *The Courier and Argus*, 27 May 1915.

[48] Ibid., 25 May 1915.

[49] 4th Battalion War Diary, Appendix No. 3 (May casualties), BWRA.

[50] Andrews, *Haunting Years*, p. 131.

[51] *The Courier and Argus*, 25 May 1915.

[52] *The People's Journal*, 22 May 1915.

[53] *The Courier and Argus*, 28 May 1915.

[54] Ibid. 27 May 1915.

[55] *The Courier and Argus*, 20 May 1915.

[56] Sidney Steven Letters, 10 May 1915.

[57] *The Courier and Argus*, 7 July 1915.

[58] Ibid. 9 July 1915; Diary of Alex Thomson, 23 July 1915.

[59] Andrews, *Haunting Years*, p. 143.

[60] Ibid. p. 146.

[61] *The Courier and Argus*, 20 July 1915.

[62] Andrews, *Haunting Years*, p. 150.

Chapter Five
Dundee's Dark Hour
The Battle of Loos and its Aftermath

Men are killed: the Battalion goes on.

- Lieutenant-Colonel Harry Walker, C.O.

'A Grand Advance but at Great Cost': The Battle of Loos, 25 September 1915

By September 1915, there was an increasing sense among both the 4th Black Watch and the Dundee press that something was approaching. Captain Patrick Duncan suggested in a letter home that 'things may be going a little quicker shortly', which was echoed by Sidney Steven when he wrote on 13 September that 'you may expect news soon in the papers from our part of the line. To tell you the truth I think we are going to be in for a very hot time of it very shortly'.[1] Clearly, the men of the 'Fourth' were aware of an impending battle, but knew few details regarding what kind of fight it would be, or the involvement of their battalion. Liddel Hart argued in his influential work on the First World War that 'in early September the "back of the Front" in France was seething with rumours'.[2] This would certainly seem to be the case, and there is a shared sense of growing tension in the main first-hand accounts of Alex Thomson, Sidney Steven and the Dundee newspapers as the summer of 1915 waned. Throughout July and August mixed reports had appeared in the newspapers ranging from the calculation of casualty figures – 'Where the shrapnel takes its toll' on 3 July – to the printing of numerous Joseph Lee poems and of 'twenty-five days with the Fourth', in which the Fighter Writers filled in the Dundee newspapers with as much information about what they were doing during this relatively quiet summer.[3] Yet the men of the 'Fourth' had known, and the people of Dundee were probably well informed enough to guess, that something was coming. Alex Thomson was just one of the soldiers who noticed that 'all the work we had put in at trench building was not for nothing'.[4] The day that The Black Watch's 4th Battalion and the civilians back in Dundee had been anticipating for months finally arrived on 25 September 1915: the Battle of Loos.

Historians have contested the Battle of Loos furiously over the decades following the Great War. It was a defining battle of the First World War, and when it took place in autumn 1915 it was the biggest land battle in British military history.[5] It is most famous for being the first and only time the British deployed poison gas against the enemy. Nick Lloyd offers a new and illuminating account of Loos, evaluating and reassessing the common perception that it was a battle for which the British Army was ill-prepared and went down in the annals of the First World War as a stereotypical case of 'bungling'.[6] In his book *Flowers of the Forest* (2007), Trevor Royle argued that the one fact relating to it upon which historians agree is that it was an 'unnecessary and unwanted battle': indeed, *Loos: The Unwanted Battle* serves as the title for a book on the offensive by Gordon Corrigan (2006).[7] It is not the concern of this study to cast aspersions on the success or failure of the Battle of Loos, but to document and analyse the role of the 4th Black Watch within the history of the wider battle. However, perceptions of how the newspapers, and more importantly the soldiers, viewed the battle will be employed and considered as a resource for interpreting how the Battle of Loos was judged at the time.

Wauchope recognised that Loos would never be remembered as a 'particularly glorious page' in British military history, but that the Scottish divisions who took a part in it regardless were to 'cover themselves with glory'.[8] The Battle of Loos included a total of 45 Scottish battalions of the British Army, including the Bareilly Brigade, of which the 4th Battalion of The Black Watch was a part.[9] On 25 September, the 'Fourth' stood at 'only 423 bayonets as opposed to 900', showing that the battalion had lost more than half of the men who had stood on the shores of France only seven months previously.[10] Most notably, only thirteen of the 21 officers with the battalion were of the original contingent of the 'Fourth'. The Battles of Neuve Chapelle and Aubers Ridge were two great events that had burst holes amongst the ranks of the 'Fourth', with many men dead and others still recovering at home or critically wounded. Additionally, everyday casualties during trench duties, as well as those caused by sickness, had worn down the battalion during the course of 1915. Thus the 'Fourth' stood as a somewhat beleaguered and affected group of men from the city of Dundee, but a ready and a proud one.

The scene of the autumn offensive was between La Bassée and Arras, of which the British share was the Battle of Loos. The main objective of the attack was to draw the enemy reserves from the districts east of Loos and to distract the attention of the German staff. In many ways this made the role of the 'Fourth' a secondary one, but nevertheless important and ambitious. The plan was to take the familiar terrain of Aubers Ridge: the 2nd Black Watch on the left flank; the 4th Black Watch on the right; and the 69th Punjabis in the centre, with two other brigades in support of the two flanks.[11] Due to uncut wire holding up support during the battle, the two Black Watch battalions were left exposed to the enemy. As shall be seen in the progress of this chapter, such failure in arrangements would result in heavy losses for the 'Fourth', which were, to be blunt, horrendous.

The most detailed account of the battle's proceedings is found in Wauchope's history of The Black Watch during the First World War. In addition, Colonel Harry Walker's field service diary, dated 24 August 1915, shows that the plans for the 4th Black Watch were to attack its assigned part of the enemy trenches first, then proceed to capture the fire trench and support trenches, before consolidating that position, with a view to further advances.[12] Zero hour on the morning of 25 September was at 5.50am when, in accordance with Walker's schedule, the British bombardment opened and a large mine successfully exploded under the enemy's position in front of the 2nd Black Watch, and chlorine gas and smoke were released. However, as documented by Major-General Wauchope, the wind was 'not favourable for the employment of gas' as it was light and constantly changing, and consequently many British and Indian troops were put out of action before they had time to put on their gas masks.[13] At 6am, also according to Walker's plan, 'C' and 'D' Companies of the 4th Battalion, The Black Watch, mounted the parapet. William Linton Andrews, who was with one of the leading companies, explained that due to the release of gas and the enemy bombing on the front trench, the initial advance took place under 'confusing' conditions.[14] Major

Tarleton, the battalion's esteemed Adjutant, was leading the men and was badly wounded in the face whilst standing encouraging them to move forwards. Captain Patrick Duncan, standing on top of the parapet urging his men forwards, was hit and fell into the trench, severely injuring his legs.[15] He later wrote a letter stating he '[had] everything to be thankful for.'[16] Indeed, the attack launched by the 'Fourth' instantly met with steady rifle fire and suffered badly from the offset, and 'officers and men fell on every side'.[17] Enemy fire only increased in volume and intensity, and German artillery caused casualties to increase substantially in a very short space of time. Wauchope's regimental history of The Black Watch during the war includes a description of the 4th Battalion's initial advance: 'Men stopped in their stride to pitch forward and lie motionless on the ground. Many others were wounded, and either lay where they fell or, if still able to walk, struggled on until their strength gave out and they too fell'.[18] His account is particularly poignant when it is considered that he was himself taking part in the battle on the other side of the Bareilly Brigade with the 2nd Battalion.

Despite heavy fire, the leading companies of the 'Fourth' had managed, 'magnificently led by their officers and non-commissioned officers,' to secure the German front line, and had 'swept forward' to capture the support trenches.[19] At the same time, the British artillery lengthened its range to cut off German reinforcements, and those left in the trenches were captured or, if they showed resistance, silenced. By this time, 'A' and 'B' Companies, along with Lieutenant-Colonel Harry Walker, Major Tosh and his staff had also mounted the parapet and were advancing across No Man's Land. Sergeant Addison, who wrote the entry about the battle for the Battalion War Diary, described the German shrapnel shellfire as very 'accurate and clever', creating a 'screen of shrapnel' to separate the first and second contingents of the 'Fourth' from joining each other.[20] They came across some very heavy German artillery fire 'which now swept that area and the captured front line', and Major Tosh was hit by a bullet.[21] He was at once lifted up by Sergeant Petrie, who was carrying the Major to cover, before Tosh was shot again and this time killed. Petrie later received the Military Medal for his attempt to save the high-ranking officer so well admired amongst his troops. Despite these difficulties, all four companies of the 'Fourth' had managed to capture the enemy's second position, half a mile ahead of the German front line that 'C' and 'D' companies had already captured. 'A' and 'B' reunited with the other companies at this second position to reinforce and count their losses:

> There they occupied the trenches from which they had just driven the Germans, and made every effort to consolidate this new position. The losses had been severe, but every man in the 4th had the feeling of victory achieved, and that the assault had added further honour to his Battalion.[22]

This feeling of accomplishment, however, was not to last.

The actions of the Bareilly Brigade in general, and the 4th Black Watch in particular, had been successful, and their objectives so far achieved. However, the 4th Battalion had advanced so quickly that they had missed some enemy troops, and one-by-one the men, and in particular the officers, were picked off by a group of six snipers. Andrews argued that the task for snipers of identifying officers with the Battalion was made easy by the characteristic red hackle 'gleaming like a tropical flower in the bonnet'. After the Battle of Loos, the red hackle was issued to all men to stop snipers being able to distinguish officers from the rank-and-file.[23]

Before long, the battalion was met with further grave danger. The troops from other battalions that were supposed to protect both flanks of the Brigade were detained elsewhere, and thus the 4th Black Watch was open to counter-attacks from the enemy. Colonels Walker and Wauchope's attempts to set up artillery posts to protect the exposed flanks from enemy fire were unsuccessful due to the losses in both Black Watch battalions. The urgently needed reserves were unbearably slow in reaching them. Their ranks had been thoroughly depleted, and Wauchope noted that by this stage all the officers of the 4th Battalion had been either killed or wounded except Colonel Walker, Captain Air and Lieutenant Cunningham.[24] The overall position of the Brigade was 'exceedingly dangerous' due to the exposed flanks and the vast distance of the troops from their original position. Harry Walker was busy trying to join up with the 2/8th Gurkhas, the only unit from the Garhwal Brigade that had managed to advance alongside the right flank, but it was an increasingly precarious situation, as the enemy was fast amassing their reserves in preparation for a counter-attack. On either flank of the Bareilly Brigade, enemy troops were gathering reinforcements facing the 4th and 2nd Battalions of The Black Watch, and the situation grew increasingly ominous as communications between both battalions and Brigade Headquarters were cut off. The efforts of the Signal Section under Sergeant Gardiner to re-establish communications were in vain. The situation appeared hopeless.

German bombing attacks began at around 11.00am, and increased in number; the 4th Battalion had already been reduced to around half its strength by this stage. Unsurprisingly, the advance was called off, and Harry Walker gave the command that the 4th Black Watch should occupy and consolidate the captured German trenches, and do all they could in preparation to resist a counter-attack. German artillery opened fire prior to the counter-attack so that Brigade Headquarters had no awareness as to what was happening on the battleground. With the wires cut, runners were instead sent out to attempt to deliver messages, but each one was shot down and so none could get through. As the shellfire intensified, it became clear that a counter-attack was due at any moment, and it was all the officers and men could do to strengthen their position. Gradually, 'the inevitable happened' and the counter-attack began, with the enemy forces winning back their lost ground with 'great steadiness'.[25] After holding out 'for as long as possible', the 'Fourth' were pushed back from their position, making stand after stand to halt and fire at the enemy as they retired, inflicting as much damage on the German attackers as possible. While contributing to the enemy's death toll, however, they were accumulating their own.[26]

Recognising the severity of the situation, and fearing that the ground that had been so deftly gained would be irrevocably lost, Colonel Walker, 'who throughout the battle had conducted operations with great valour and coolness', sought a solution to the lack of reserves available, but they were not contactable due to the breakdown of communications.[27] Rather than delegate the task to a soldier of lesser rank, Walker set out himself in a 'gallant attempt' to cross No Man's Land and to reach the Brigadier-General to demand reinforcements for his men. It was not long before he was shot and mortally wounded. He died two days later in an army hospital.

Meanwhile, the enemy bombardment continued relentlessly, whilst the 4th Battalion's bombs had run out and, according to Sergeant

Addison's account in the Battalion War Diary, many of the men's rifles had become unworkable 'owing to clogging up with mud'.[28] The remaining men were running short of ammunition, and continuing their retreat had no choice but to leave the last of the land they had so successfully captured that morning, and returned across No Man's Land to reoccupy the British lines, which they reached by 11.30am Wauchope records that the men of the 'Fourth' were still recognised for their 'manful' and 'brave' attempts, receiving the highest praise from Brigade and Divisional Commanders. Since the main objective of the Bareilly Brigade was not to occupy ground but to draw German reserves from 'more vital parts' of the battlefield, and therefore giving assistance to British divisions elsewhere in the field, it had done much to do so. The summary of the role of the 'Fourth' in the wider context of the 'Battle of Loos' was that it had achieved its objectives, despite having lost the ground gained in the field. That there was no shame for the 'Fourth' is shown as Sergeant Addison finished his account of the battle for the Battalion's official war diary with the following:

> IT HAD BEEN A GRAND ADVANCE BUT AT GREAT COST.
>
> We had forced the enemy to turn on many of his heaviest pieces against us, and forced him to bring up very large reserves. Attacks were made at other parts of the line that day and the enemy's reserves had to be drawn off.[29]

However, it was not only the loss of the captured ground that the remaining men of the 4th Black Watch lamented. Of the twenty officers and 420 men who had taken part in the attack, nineteen officers and 230 men were killed or wounded in the space of one morning. The men and officers of the 'Fourth' had been injured or killed side by side, and by the end of 25 September 1915 it was almost unrecognisable. It is a meaningful coincidence, then, that the native pronunciation of 'Loos' is 'loss'.

The Solemn City: Dundee and its Response to Loos

To state merely that the consequences of the Battle of Loos had a very profound effect on the city of Dundee would be a grave understatement. When considering Dundonian soldiers in the various regiments of the British Expeditionary Force that fought at Loos, rarely was a family unaffected by the severe losses suffered on 25 September 1915. The devastation of the 4th Black Watch was particularly poignant in Dundee civilians' perceptions of the war from that point onwards. Indeed, to this day, the beacon of the granite monument erected on the summit of the Dundee Law is lit every year on 25 September as a memorial to the Dundee men lost during that battle. The impression that the Battle of Loos left upon the city of Dundee is hugely important in understanding local perceptions of the war. Because of the heavy depletion of ranks among the 'Fourth', the extensive newspaper coverage that was available to the city could not hope to continue in the way it had done before. As the remaining ranks of the 4th Black Watch attempted to recuperate and to understand what had happened to them, the people of Dundee, who had been notified that a 'push' was expected any day now, were waiting anxiously both for official news from the Press Bureau, and the personal letters that were expected to be published in the newspapers. The Dundee newspapers' response to the Battle of Loos will be examined in this section, revealing the profound effect that the battle had upon the city. Prior to this, however, a brief representation of the soldiers' reactions to the Battle as found in the first-hand accounts is necessary.

For the one unwounded officer and 199 men who emerged unharmed from the battlefield near Manquissant, the effects of Loos were far more immediate than for those in Dundee who, for a short time, remained ignorant of what had occurred on the Western Front. William Linton Andrews described the Battle of Loos as 'a day of tragedy' for the Battalion, but argued that it proved 'the old battalion could fight better than ever'.[30] However, he lamented that he had lost many of his good friends that day, but mentioned that there was little time to mourn, for the reorganisation of the Battalion was necessary. Alex Thomson did not actually take part in the battle, and on 25 September he was on his way back from Le Havre down the La Bassée Road to Headquarters, and observed 'a constant stream' of Red Cross wagons passing by full of wounded men. Hearing the boom of artillery to the south, Thomson gathered that he was returning on the day of the great 'advance'. Once at headquarters, the immediacy of the information reaching him and his companions is made obvious from this entry in his journal:

We walked quickly to Headquarters to learn how things were going and found everyone in great excitement. The "Fourth" were great! We had charged first and had the Germans on the run out in the open. We had taken trench after trench – nothing could stand against the "Fourth". Shortly afterwards a new note crept in with the reports. The Battalion was cut off – a whole company had surrendered – we were retreating and were back to our own second line – no, we still hold the first line – and so on.[31]

All afternoon Thomson hid from the rain, trying to find out as much about what was happening as possible. In the afternoon, he reported someone arriving with 'the awful news that Lieutenant Cunningham was in the support trench line with 53 men – all that remained of the Battalion'.[32] The remaining men were to return that night to find as many other men as they could and bring them back the following morning, which brought the final strength of the 'Fourth' to 212 men. As the 'stragglers' returned during the course of 26 September, Thomson observed that 'it would have moved anyone to tears to see that little band of mud covered men lined up on parade and to note the frequency with which names were unanswered at the roll-call'.[33] Thomson's own Company, 'D', had suffered the most, being the first over the parapet, and could muster only 49 men. 'Could we be blamed if our spirits dropped to zero?' Thomson enquired rhetorically in his diary, pointing out that nearly all of the 'best of the Battalion' had disappeared, particularly among the ranks of the officers.[34] There was no time to mourn the dead of the Battalion, and arrangements had to be made at once among the confusion of the post-Loos haze.

Back in Dundee, a confused picture of what had happened on the Western Front was beginning to emerge in the closing days of September, although it was not until early October before a clearer idea of the gravity of the situation was made known. Bruce Pandrich condemned the ability of the Dundee newspapers to report accurately the 'virtual destruction' of a section of the city's population.[35] Pandrich argues that 'at first the newspapers in Dundee offered a very conventional interpretation of the events at Loos', but correctly identifies a growing 'disquiet' as reports gradually seeping in from the men of the 'Fourth' clashed with the official ones forwarded from the

Press Bureau.[36] Pandrich interprets this 'disquiet' as the uncomfortable guilt felt by the Dundee newspapers for their seemingly deliberate skewed reporting of the battle. This does not appear to be a realistic assessment of the Dundee newspapers' reportage following Loos. During the days immediately succeeding Loos, though, only national headlines were available to print in the provincial press, which portrayed a great victory. The *Courier and Argus* on 27 September, for instance, reported the 'great offensive' as a huge triumph for British and French troops, advancing up to three miles and the capture of 20,000 prisoners.[37] However, this was printed when little real information from the Front was available. When the full effect of the battle became clear, the tone of the newspapers changed dramatically.

Once letters from the Front eventually reached Dundee, newspaper reports of council meetings in Dundee record the civilians 'living under the shadow of perhaps the blackest cloud that we have ever experienced' and report that 'great distress [has] been brought to Dundee by the news of the last few days'.[38] Even the patriotic *People's Journal*, which held the sentiment that 'it is sweet and glorious to die for one's country' close to its heart, referred to the consequences of Loos as 'Dundee's Dark Hour'.[39] The men's lives were described as having 'passed in the din and conflict of battle, amidst carnage more fearful than the world has ever known', referring to the 'harrowing' sacrifices made by Dundee's men.[40] The first newspaper reports of Loos are altogether different from those published after Neuve Chapelle and Aubers Ridge.[41] The *Courier* on 29 September admits that 'the news to hand is fragmentary', and openly refers to Loos as a victory, but also warns the public that 'the latest blow sustained by the battalion is the most serious of all'.[42] The *Dundee Advertiser*, also printing its first reports on Wednesday 29 September, describes the Loos casualty list as 'the most melancholy which the 4th Black Watch have yet furnished'.[43] On 2 October *The People's Journal* first reported the battle, instinctively depicting it as a glorious victory, stating that '[Dundee's] sons have covered themselves with undying glory'.[44] The first report of the *Journal* appears to be more of a dramatic homage to the men of the 'Fourth' than a serious journalistic attempt, but its subsequent issues do present a clearer picture. As the ensuing days progressed, photographs, poems, elegies and letters from the front covered at least one page in each of the Dundee newspapers until well into October. The men of the 'Fourth' expressed that they were happy with the reportage of the newspapers, as Harvey Steven wrote to his parents stating: 'We have seen the "Advertiser" and the "Journal" both of which give a good account of the 4th'.[45]

Bruce Pandrich is not so positive about the ability of the Dundee press, and states that the newspapers reported the consequences of the Battle of Loos with 'a conscious manipulation which went with the attempts to report the war in optimistic terms'.[46] Both sides of this argument can be examined regarding the reportage of the death of Colonel Harry Walker, with whom the Dundee newspapers had shown a great interest and pride in since the onset of war almost precisely one year previously. Pandrich asserts that 'Walker's death was hedged by euphemism', and his example manipulated as a recruitment ploy, 'used to exhort young men to go and fight'.[47] Although Harry Walker's demise was recorded under the headline 'A HERO'S DEATH', with a fervently patriotic 'IN MEMORIAM' article in *The People's Journal*, the circumstances under which Walker died attempting single-handedly to retrieve reserves were indubitably brave. His death was documented in the national as well as the local Dundee press, but not nearly so much information is available from *The Scotsman*, which states plainly that Walker 'fell wounded in the abdomen, [and] died in hospital'.[48] The detail of the local press was more dedicated to commemorating Walker and the other lost men, and published multiple eulogies to his memory and bravery in the field. Yet sensitivity following Loos is also prevalent, as can be ascertained from Harvey Steven's more graphic account of Walker's death: 'He lay wounded in a shell hole for several hours, with a sniper potting at him the whole time'.[49] Although not published fully in the Dundee newspapers, the actual circumstances of Walker's death do little to detract from an accurate portrayal of casualties of Loos. Walker's death was not hidden from his family; Harvey Steven specified that Mrs Walker already knew the full story of what happened to her husband.[50] Detailed descriptions of British deaths in newspapers would have seemed unnecessary and disrespectful, a reasonable deduction even by modern-day standards.[51] The people of Dundee may not have been told the whole story of the soldiers' suffering, but by inspecting official records and first-hand accounts cross-referenced with newspaper reports it would appear that the majority of reports by the Dundee press were faithful accounts of the 4th Black Watch.

Due to the heavy officer casualties at the Battle of Loos, whose testaments of fallen men were commonplace in the Dundee newspapers, there were not nearly as many letters from the Front concerning deaths within the rank-and-file in the 'Fourth' which were available for the newspapers to print. Only one officer, Lieutenant Cunningham, was uninjured, which meant there could be very few condolence letters to families from officers who commanded a fallen man's company and had known the casualty well. Proportionately, the officer class suffered more than the rank-and-file at Loos, which shook the structure of the battalion itself and the way the papers received news about 'Dundee's Own'. Thus reportage of individual circumstances adopted a far more simplistic nature in likeness to the national newspapers, for example: 'Private Joseph McLaughlan (killed) was a millworker, resident in Lochee, and employed in the Camperdown Jute Works'.[52] Articles regarding the losses sustained at Loos focused almost entirely on the collective battalion as opposed to individual casualties, at least until more information was received later in 1915 and even into 1916. The readiness of Dundee's newspapers earlier in the year to report the circumstances surrounding the deaths of the rank-and-file would suggest that the lack of information available to the press following Loos was the main obstacle, rather than an unwillingness to present a realistic picture of things as Pandrich suggests. There were simply not enough soldiers left with the 4th Battalion who were capable of writing detailed accounts of their comrades' deaths.

Where possible, the newspapers described accurately the actions of the 4th Black Watch during the battle, fully acknowledging that the Battalion had to retreat and give up the ground it had worked so hard, and sacrificed so much, to gain. One letter received from a member of the 4th depicted the order to retreat as being 'received with deep regret, tempered with a feeling of satisfaction that the Fourth was the last company of the brigade to retire'.[53] As mentioned in the previous chapter, great solace was found in the fact that the 'Fourth' had achieved their main objective, to draw out German reserves, regardless of the fact that they had lost their captured ground. This achievement, and the deep respect shown to the battalion by the brigade and division chiefs, appeared as something of a consolation prize to compensate for the loss of enemy territory and loss of men more generally. In this regard at least, Pandrich is correct in his analysis of the motivation of the Dundee newspapers by stating that 'the public confidence was destroyed and somehow the newspapers had to salvage some psychology of survival out of the evidence of despair and hopelessness'.[54] Indeed, a prevailing aspect of the Dundee newspapers during the city's grief is the promotion of, and a belief in, a sense of community and collectiveness. In their sorrow, the people of the city came together. Memorial services for the fallen were held across Dundee. On 7 October, the newspapers reported a service held at St Mary's Parish Church, the proceedings of which revealed a collective feeling that 'Dundee has been stirred by the avalanche of death which swept over officers and men of the 4th Black Watch', accounting for the huge congregation present, which filled the church, to commemorate the fallen.[55] Much in the way that the 'Fourth' was symbolic as 'Dundee's Own' of all the men of Dundee who were fighting in all corners of the First World War, so too was the memorial service symbolic of the awful quantity of Dundee life that had been lost in September 1915. The Last Post was sounded at the close of the service, and the Lord Provost aptly described Dundee as 'a city of sorrow, but a city very proud in her sorrow'.[56]

Whilst the citizens of Dundee were coming to terms with the loss following the Battle of Loos, expressed and concentrated within the pages of its newspapers, the remaining men of the 'Fourth' were recuperating in France. Once again, the concept of the newspapers bridging the gap between soldier and civilian between France and Dundee comes into play, and tributes paid in the form of poetry published in the Dundee newspapers became an important way to work through the grief of the time. An example of this acknowledgement of the service of the 'Fourth' is clear in the following:

> Lads o' valour, lads o' grit,
>
> Lads wha's frames are strongly knit,
>
> Lads wha strike hard whom they hit,
>
> Are in the Fourth.

The 'Great Push' found them tae the fore,

Like their sires in days of yore.

'Marmalade!' Eh, what a roar!

    Cam' frae the Fourth.

They cared not for the rifles' spit,

They were oot tae dae their bit,

They've proved that they are lads o' grit,

    Oor gallant Fourth.[57]

The deeply instilled sense of connection between civilian and soldier is prominent in poetry of this type, exemplified by protective language such as 'oor gallant Fourth'. Gradually, the men of the battalion shared their own experiences of the aftermath of Loos. This is particularly prevalent in the case of the burial of the 'father' of the 4th Black Watch, Harry Walker. As mentioned throughout this book, both Walker and Major Tosh were renowned characters in Dundee. Their burial in a small orchard at Pont du Hem 'within range of the guns' was shared by an unnamed man of the 'Fourth' who sent the following description to *The Courier and Argus*:

> What a difference to-day looking around the ranks of dishevelled, warworn, sad men compared to the boisterous enthusiasm of the 1100 who paraded in Dudhope Square that afternoon in February…I remember yet the pride in the Colonel's eye that day…and the cheery smile of the Major.[58]

The grief felt by the battalion at the loss of their Commanding Officer was palpable. Alex Thomson, who had just returned to the Front as the 4th Battalion's tragic role in the Battle of Loos was coming to an end, describes the 'grief of the whole Battalion' at the knowledge that when the Colonel was brought in after suffering on the battlefield for hours, he died two days later in hospital. Thomson describes the scene of his and Major Tosh's funeral in his diary:

> The saddest task any regiment can have is to bury its colonel, and when the First and Second in command Colonel Walker and

Major Tosh were laid together in a neat little graveyard at Pont du Hem everyone present (all that remained of the Battalion) was deeply moved. The bodies were carried from the road between a double row of men who presented arms as the little procession passed, and so to their last resting place. The service was short and simple but beautifully sincere.[59]

The Commanding Officer of the 2nd Black Watch, Major-General Wauchope, had become good friends with Harry Walker and in his account of the 'Fourth' dedicates an entire page to his memory. He noted the tragic poetry of the fact that Walker was killed 'in action at the head of his men, commanding the Battalion that he loved so well', attributing much of the success of the Battalion to their undoubted love and loyalty towards him, that had earned the 'Fourth' the 'high esteem of all soldiers and civilians'.[60] If there was ever an example of the respect that the men of the 4th Black Watch held for their officers, and in particular Harry Walker, it was exemplified in the loss of all save one of them at the Battle of Loos in September 1915.

'Poor battered old battalion': Aftermath and Amalgamation

Due to the heavy depletion in its ranks, the remnant of the 4th Black Watch was split into two companies and temporarily attached to the 2nd Black Watch, a battalion familiar to the 'Fourth' and commanded by their dead commander's friend, Lieutenant-Colonel Wauchope. The temporarily amalgamated battalion, which had comprised two of the units during their onslaught at Loos, was not given much respite, and moved on to La Gorgue. This movement saw for the first time the collection of the two Regular battalions, the 1st and 2nd, two Territorial battalions, the 4th and 5th, and two Service battalions, the 8th and 9th of The Black Watch, who came together to uphold the tradition of the regiment 'most worthily'.[61] The defence of the 'little hill' of Givenchy was entrusted to two British battalions, the 1st Seaforth Highlanders and the 2nd and 4th Black Watch battalion, around which area the Black Watch battalion took over the trenches on 1 October. The duties here were 'arduous', with relentless shelling and a 'constant battle [...] between the German and Black Watch snipers'.[62] Wauchope boasted proudly that 'nothing could exceed the energy and power of leadership' displayed by the two remaining company commanders of the 'Fourth' and, because of progressive mining from the German side, the defence of this area was hard-going and very dangerous.

By mid-October, after defending Givenchy despite being so short of men, the 4th and 2nd Black Watch were finally allowed to rest in billets, where ranks were once again built up by new drafts of officers and men, as well as those from the 4th Battalion who had since recovered from wounds suffered at Loos.[63] The 2nd Black Watch was sufficiently restored and reorganised as a complete unit and, in early November, the 2nd Battalion – 'those wonderful regulars' as Andrews recalled them – were ordered to leave France for Mesopotamia.[64] On 4 November 1915, Lieutenant-Colonel Wauchope issued the following farewell order:

> It is with great regret that I leave the 4th Black Watch. I wish the Battalion was to come with the 2nd Battalion, and that we could continue fighting side by side as we have done for the past nine months [...] On behalf of the 2nd Battalion I wish the 1/4th all good fortune. I can wish the Battalion nothing better than they continue to fight in the same gallant way that distinguished their attack on September 25th.[65]

Wauchope paid tribute to the bonds of friendship between the 2nd and 4th Battalions of The Black Watch, stating that 'the many hardships and test of battles shared together had only served to knit this friendship all the more firmly'.[66] He emphasised the extraordinary courage of the two leading officers of the 4th Black Watch, Lieutenant T. Stevenson and Lieutenant R. C. Cunningham, the latter of whom was the only officer to make it through Loos unscathed, for their excellent command during 'this most difficult time'. Both officers were subsequently – and probably consequently – awarded the Military Cross for gallantry in France; Lieutenant Stevenson was wounded twice in 1916 and was killed in action in 1917; and Lieutenant Cunningham was also later killed in action.

After leaving the 2nd Black Watch, the 'Fourth' was still not strong enough to act as an independent unit, and was attached to the 44th Brigade, 15th Division, IV Corps, with which it spent November and December, before being withdrawn from the line and given a period of rest. The 'Fourth' was then to join the 51st (Highland) Territorial Division which was by the end of 1915 at Fricourt in the Somme area. At the end of the year, the 'Fourth' had received many drafts of officers and men and was 'almost up to fighting strength', with a fourth company formed on Christmas Day. The battalion also gained a new Commanding Officer, Lieutenant-Colonel G. McL. Sceales of the 1st Argyll and Sutherland Highlanders, who took over the command from the acting C.O., Captain R.C. Cunningham.[67] The men of the 'Fourth', including Andrews, soon found faith in this new leader, and Major Rogers stated in *The People's Journal* that he believed Sceales to be 'the right man to replace our lamented Commander, Harry Walker'.[68] Under him the 'poor battered old battalion' was once more made fit to fight.[69] On 1 January 1916, the Battalion consisted of 28 officers and 685 men, who were entrained at Lillers before reaching billets at Rainneville, about seven miles from Amiens, and formed part of the 154th Brigade of the 51st (Highland Division). This Brigade was composed of the 4th and 5th Black Watch, the 4th Seaforth Highlanders and the 4th Cameron Highlanders. Spending January and the beginning of February training and resting, the Battalion was also inspected by Brigade and Divisional Commanders. It was while the troops were here that the future of the 4th Black Watch was decided.

On 16 February 1916, the 4th Battalion War Diary records an interview between Major Muir who, in the absence of Lieutenant-Colonel Sceales, was the Commanding Officer of the 5th Black Watch, and Sir Neville Macready, the Adjutant-General, at the General Headquarters regarding the proposed amalgamation of the 4th Black Watch with its neighbouring battalion, the 5th (Forfarshire) Battalion The Black Watch. The Adjutant-General informed the two officers that the decision had been made 'either to split up these two Battalions and draft them to other units of the Black Watch or to amalgamate them into one Battalion'.[70] Major Muir stated he 'was personally much against either of the two alternatives', but decided that the men of the battalion would probably prefer the amalgamation. Therefore, it was decided that this would be the way forward for both Territorial battalions, which would join the 118th Brigade, 39th Division, which had just arrived in France.

On 25 February 1915, the 4th Battalion The Black Watch

('Dundee's Own') marched its last as an independent unit through ten kilometres of a 'blinding snowstorm' to Renescure near St Omer so the amalgamation could take place. The weather was so bad along the road that the Battalion had to find some billets in which to wait out the weather, which improved by the end of February. On 7 March proceedings for the amalgamation of the two battalions to become a new unit, to be known as the 4/5th Black Watch, became official. As shown in William Linton Andrews's account, the general consensus of the soldiers was that the men of the 'Fourth' were disappointed with the arrangement:

> We were by no means pleased at the prospect of amalgamation with the 5th. Our chief constable, Sergeant Watt, said he would be ashamed to be found dead in the 5th, but the alternative would have been to be split up into drafts for other Black Watch battalions - which we should have hated - and anyway we had no choice in the matter.[71]

Much as Andrews changed his mind about his new comrades when he had first joined the 'Fourth' in August 1914, he and his comrades soon changed their minds and the 4/5th Battalion became 'very happy together' and made 'an exceedingly good battalion'.[72] Proceeding on to do good work at the Somme, Arras and Ypres, the Territorial men of Dundee – now with the Territorial men of Angus – would continue fighting for King and country. Once formed as the 4/5th Battalion The Black Watch, Andrews acted as secretary to the new Colonel, keeping the Battalion War Diary and writing articles for the newspapers back home, particularly the *Dundee Advertiser*. Even after it was technically no longer 'Dundee's Own', Andrews states that 'then, as later, we were upheld by a feeling of spiritual oneness with the people of our own homes. Dundee was proud of us'.[73] Since Alex Thomson had returned to Dundee after receiving a commission, Captain Patrick Duncan was at home wounded, Joseph Lee became a prisoner of war, and both Sidney and Harvey Steven were dead, Andrews's is the only first-hand account that depicts the actions of the original members of the 4th Black Watch after their amalgamation with the 5th Battalion. Although his experience of the war from 1916 onwards was mainly behind a desk, the last of the 'Fighter-Writers' still retained a feeling of devotion to The Black Watch and, more specifically, the battalion with which he was once so very reluctant to be associated. Certainly, the individual identity of the 'Fourth' was largely preserved, perhaps partly due to the promise of an important concession that was offered at the unhappy decision for amalgamation. Andrews recalls accurately that 'we were promised that whatever changes were made the 4th and 5th would go home after the War as two battalions, not one'.[74]

Thus ends the story of the 4th Battalion The Black Watch, ('Dundee's Own') as an independent unit until it was re-established on Armistice Day, 11 November 1918.

NOTES

[1]   Letter from Captain Patrick Duncan, University of Dundee Archives, MS 106/1/9; Sidney Steven letters, 13 September 1915.

[2]   B. Liddel Hart, *History of the First World War* (London: Pan Books Ltd., 1972), p. 193.

[3]   *The People's Journal*, especially 3 July; 8 August 1915.

[4]   Diary of Alex Thomson, 2 September 1915.

[5]   Nick Lloyd, *Loos 1915* (Stroud: Tempus, 2006), p. 13.

[6]   Ibid. pp. 14-15.

[7]   Royle, *Flowers of the Forest*, p. 83.

[8]   Wauchope, p. 15.

[9]   Young, *Forgotten Scottish Voices*, p. 141.

[10] Wauchope, p. 15.

[11] Ibid., p. 16.

[12] Lt-Col. Harry Walker, Field Service Book: Operation Order No. 5, 24 August 1915, Black Watch Regimental Archive MS 0296.

[13] Wauchope, p. 17.

[14] Andrews, *Haunting Years*, p. 160.

[15] Battalion War Diary, Appendix referring to the Battle of Loos.

[16] Captain Patrick Duncan, Letter [date unknown], University of Dundee Archives, MS 106/1/9: Letters from Captain Patrick Duncan to his family, 1914-1918.

[17] Wauchope, p. 17.

[18] Ibid. p. 17.

[19] Ibid. p. 17.

[20] Battalion War Diary, p. 9.

[21] Ibid. p. 18.

[22] Ibid. p. 18

[23] Andrews, *Haunting Years*, p. 162.

[24] Ibid. p. 162.

[25] Diary of Alex Thomson, 25 September 1915.

[26] Regimental War Diary, 25 September 1915, p. 10.

[27] Wauchope, p. 20.

[28] Regimental War Diary, 25 September 1915, p. 10.

[29] Ibid.

[30] Andrews, *Haunting Years*, p. 164.

[31] Diary of Alex Thomson, 25 September 1915.

[32] Ibid.

[33] Ibid.

[34] Ibid.

[35] Pandrich, p. 128.

[36] Ibid. p. 135.

[37] *The Courier and Argus*, 27 September 1915.

[38] *Dundee Advertiser*, 1 October 1915; *The Courier and Argus*, 2 October 1915.

[39] *The People's Journal*, 2 October 1915.

[40] *Dundee Advertiser*, 1 October 1915.

[41] *Dundee Advertiser*, 7 October 1915.

[42] *The Courier and Argus*, 29 September 1915.

[43] *Dundee Advertiser*, 29 September 1915.

[44] *The People's Journal*, 2 October 1915.

[45] Steven letters, 5 October 1915.

[46] Pandrich, pp. 140-1.

[47] Ibid. p. 140

[48] *The Scotsman*, 30 September 1915.

[49] Steven letters, 4 October 1915.

[50] Ibid.

[51] Faber, p. 24.

[52] *The People's Journal*, 2 October 1915.

[53] *The Courier and Argus*, 9 November 1915.

[54] Pandrich, p. 126

[55] *The Courier and Argus*, 7 October 1915.

56. *Dundee Advertiser*, 7 October 1915.

57. W. D. M., 'Oor Gallant Fourth', *The People's Journal*, 16 October 1915.

58. *The Courier and Argus*, 4 October 1915.

59. Diary of Alex Thomson, 28 September 1915.

60. Wauchope, p. 21.

61. Ibid. p. 22.

62. Ibid. p. 22

63. Ibid. p. 23

64. Andrews, *Haunting Years*, p. 165.

65. 4th Battalion War Diary, 1916. Appendix 1.

66. Wauchope, p. 23.

67. Ibid.

68. *The People's Journal*, 5 February 1916.

69. Andrews, *Haunting Years*, pp. 165-166.

70. Battalion War Diary, Appendix. 16 February, 1916 (Rainneville, Somme).

71. Andrews, *Haunting Years*, p. 187.

72. Ibid. p. 187.

73. Ibid. p. 182.

74. Ibid. p. 187.

Chapter Six
'I Am Quite Content With This Life'
The Story of Two 'Dundee's Own' Brothers

This book has attempted to demonstrate the human experience of the 'Fourth' through a range of first-hand, contemporary accounts. So far, however, it has omitted an extraordinary case study: a collection of letters that encapsulates the story, depicts the experience and humanises both positive and negative aspects of the 4th Black Watch's year-long expedition.[1] The authors of these letters were two brothers from Dundee, Sidney and Harvey Steven, who were both officers in the 4th Black Watch, though not at the same time. Sidney (see Plate 13), a chartered accountant in Dundee, enlisted with the 'Fourth' four months prior to the outbreak of war, whilst his elder brother Harvey was a solicitor in Stirling who joined the Scottish Horse, before obtaining a commission in his brother's battalion. Harvey would arrive to join 'Dundee's Own' in its darkest hour, in the aftermath of the Battle of Loos in September 1915. The Steven letters allow for a parallel reading of the tale of 'Dundee's Own', and they are compelling and moving in a way that the pages of the *Advertiser*, *Courier* and *People's Journal* could never be. This last chapter of the book is dedicated to the story of Sidney and Harvey Steven as an important example that exemplifies many of the core elements this book has covered: camaraderie; officer-man relations; the role of the press; and a revisionist reading of the First World War. Rather than being mere fodder for a futile cause, Harvey and Sidney Steven recognised great importance in what they were doing. Encapsulating the highs and lows of the 4th Black Watch's experience, the brothers' story serves powerfully to depict the human side of the First World War.

When the 4th Black Watch left Dundee amongst copious celebrations across the city on 23 February 1915, Lieutenant Sidney

Steven was among them. He had trained with the battalion, and travelled with the contingent to France, first moving into the Line on 5 March as the officer in charge of No. 1 Platoon of A Company. Keen to share his experiences with his parents back in Barnhill, outside Dundee, Sidney described a wide variety of experiences at the Front, explaining this was as much for his benefit as for his parents'. Often, this meant that his descriptions did little to alleviate his parents' worry towards him, as he was detailed and often very graphic in his descriptions of battles and casualties, as shall be seen throughout this chapter. If his parents ever expressed concerns relating to his well-being, Sidney responded: 'So don't go worrying about me…what good will it do? In fact I hate to think of you worrying, so please don't do it'. However, he also liked to inform his parents of more normal, everyday instances, such as descriptions of the food they received in the battalion:

Soup: - Bovril, flavoured with Worcester sauce

Fish: - Tinned salmon with salad and mayonnaise sauce (made by Badger!)

Meat: - Mince, green peas and cabbage and new potatoes.

Sweets: - Tinned cherries, pears and peaches and cream. Stewed rhubarb, strawberries and cream.

Fruit: Apples pears oranges and cherries.

Coffee and liquers.[sic] (Not bad, eh?)

Often, Sidney tried to make his letters relatable between his experience at the Front and his parents' life at home. For example, he told the story of taking over a trench from Indian soldiers, where Sidney described his annoyance at how much noise one Indian soldier was making whilst trying to tell him about patrol duties on that part of the line. Sidney put this into terms that his parents could relate to at home: 'He jabbered away and between us we were making far too much noise, as we were only as far away from the Germans as 2 Invermark Terrace is from no. 5!'

Sidney clearly enjoyed writing letters to his parents as a therapeutic means of documenting how he felt about his experience in the war. However, as an officer, he was granted little opportunity to write letters, and many are spread over the course of a whole or even multiple days:

> I had no sooner written that when someone came in and wanted me to go and look at a yellow flag that was flying in front of the German line I looked at it through my periscope but could make nothing.........(another stop there. Now its 12.30 of the next day!)...........of it.

Sidney was to prove himself a most competent leader at the Battle of Neuve Chapelle in March 1915, but he also documented the less turbulent duties of an officer in a light-hearted and informative way. He complained regularly of having to censor his platoon's letters containing all sorts of sentiments, including: 'I read a charming proposal in one letter today...a proposal of marriage I mean!' He also documented a job he found particularly boring, which was to prepare his troops for parade:

> You sling off your 'pyjamas', then into a shirt, socks, boots and kilt and off you trot to the parade ground. "Good morning, sergeant", "Good morning, sir", "All right?", "Yes, sir but two men sick", "What's the matter with them?", "Boils on the backside, sir and a sprained foot", "All right, sergeant, fall in". He salutes and off he goes behind the platoon.

Yet Sidney also had far more difficult responsibilities, such as writing to the family of those who were killed or wounded under his leadership, such as the following published in the *Courier*:

> Your son was a fine soldier, one whom I always looked upon with pride as belonging to my platoon. In the fight he was a tower of strength to the other fellows, helping and cheering them on. A better death no man could die. His death is a great loss to our company.

As well as contributing to the more personal reportage of the war already explored in this book, Sidney went a step further, requesting in one letter that his parents visit the father of one of his men killed at Neuve Chapelle. He described the deceased as 'an excellent fellow and one whom I always respected and looked to for an example of a good soldier'. Despite often appearing detached from the emotional side of loss on the Front, Sidney was clearly affected when men close to him, particularly those in the platoon he was responsible for, were killed or injured. When his platoon sergeant MacDonald died overnight he explained that he 'didn't feel right all day'. During the advance at Auber's Ridge, Sidney's company lost between 60 and 70 men including his other sergeant: 'My other one was shot through the head when he was standing just beside me'.

There is a very clear sense of camaraderie in the letters of Sidney Steven as shown in the way he responded to casualties. He clearly thought a great deal of the men he led, as well as his admiration of his fellow officers alike. Occasionally he asked for parcels for his men, appealing to his parents to try and get societies to donate clothing to soldiers in the trenches as 'my poor devils have absolutely nothing but what they stand up in'. One officer he admired in particular was the battalion's Bomb Gun Officer, Captain Patrick, who Sidney described as 'one of the best fellows I have ever met' and infamous among the men for having a gramophone behind the lines, which he used to play 'lively tunes' to drown out the sound of German shelling. On 7 August, Sidney recorded an incident when the nearby Germans were cheering as a result of Warsaw falling, and they had put up a small Russian flag at half-mast. In response, Patrick put up a notice that would be clear to the enemy trenches, the contents of which Sidney remarked 'were not very polite'. Patrick ended the note '...and take this', before sending twenty bombs over to the German lines. With these kind of stories, the more light-hearted aspects of war can be drawn from Sidney's letters, particularly his regular enjoyment with the men of the battalion as they marched along 'singing all the well known songs'. One evening, Sidney even organised a concert:

> I felt in great form for singing so we had a concert but after about an hour some of them began to feel sleepy and wanted to turn in. I sang on lustily for a while then everyone else seemed to get a bit annoyed and let fly at me with bits of candles and anything else that they could lay their hands on! Eventually Rogers, the doctor and Ian Law got up from their straw and pounced on me. Their night attack was unsuccessful although a good struggle ensued!

Something that stands out from Sidney's – and later Harvey's – letters is the adaptation to extreme circumstances that the men of the 4th Black Watch dealt with. Shortly after the battalion left the trenches at Neuve

Chappelle, Sidney complained that the men had to lie in a quagmire in an open field filled with about six inches of water. Sidney depicted Harry Walker saying '[y]ou'll just have to make the best of it, boys' to which Sidney reflected in his letter: 'So we did.' Soon enough, Sidney would boast that he and the men would 'stick it out and think nothing of it'. In these conditions the men and officers seemed united, as shown one morning in the trenches when Sidney was called to see Lieutenant-Colonel Harry Walker in his dug-out. Sidney described the Commanding Officer of the 4th Black Watch 'picking lice out of his shirt' as he arrived, warning his mother in the letter: 'Don't go telling Mrs Walker that her husband was hunting lice at five in the morning…although it is true enough!)'. Sidney did not sugar-coat his experiences; such jovial anecdotes often shared the same letters as information about one of his fellow men being shot. What his accounts exemplify is how varied a picture the 'Fourth's' experience in France really was.

Sidney's letters to his parents also allow an insight into the accuracy of the Dundee newspapers and, even more than that, the strictness of DORA with which the first chapter of this book is concerned. Sidney was regularly complimentary about the content of the Dundee papers, expressing after Neuve Chapelle that 'all that I have read in the papers about the attack has been perfectly correct'. Sidney had no qualms whatsoever with correcting the newspaper reports, however, and corrected details he disagreed with. The Dundee newspapers stated the bombardment preceding Neuve Chapelle continued for 35 minutes. Sidney wrote specifically to correct this mistake, pointing out that it actually lasted for an hour and 45 minutes. Although an avid reader of the Dundee newspapers when these were available at the Front, Sidney told his parents expressly on numerous occasions that he did not want his letters published in them. Once, he warned that if they continued to do so then he would stop giving them any information about his actions. The fact that Sidney's parents wished to contribute their son's experience at the Front to the plethora of accounts published in the local press, with or without his permission, shows how important the culture of printing soldiers' letters in local newspapers was to the city.

On 17 March, Sidney told his parents how much the makeup of the battalion had changed since arriving in France, explaining that the

'Fourth' had lost about 140 men, but instructed his parents to 'keep this quiet'. This letter reached Dundee uncensored, and Sidney would go on to write letters that gave even more information that should, under DORA, have been strictly regulated. In a letter dated 25 March, Sidney even gave his parents details of a specific location: 'we are about 600 yards north of Neuve Chapelle…Keep that information absolutely dark'. The only words struck out, yet still legible, were 'Neuve Chapelle'. On 1 July, during the long summer between Aubers Ridge and Loos, Sidney even requested a private camera from his parents: a 'nice little one' with which he could take snapshots of his experiences at the Front. Private cameras were strictly prohibited under DORA, but his wish was granted and a small camera with some film was sent to Sidney. He sent back the finished films to be developed at home, which include a variety of photographs, many of which comprise the illustrations found in the plate section of this book. They display many things: the easy company and camaraderie amongst men (see Plates 4, 5, 6 and 7); pictures of No Man's Land that Sidney acquired by deciding to 'wander out' in broad daylight protected by long grass (Plate 8); and even a self-portrait of himself sitting in a dug-out writing a letter, presumably to his parents (Plate 13). Sidney clearly enjoyed being able to document his experience in this way, requesting more film for his camera just over a week since he acquired it, and asking his parents if they wanted him to take pictures of anything in particular: 'What about Germans at breakfast or something like that…just say the word'.

Although Sidney's descriptions of all aspects of life on the Western Front are important and fascinating, his descriptions of battle are particularly illuminating. His talent for words shows itself most pertinently when he describes, even in his earliest letters, imagery of the battlefield. Just before Neuve Chapelle, he described the sight of No Man's Land in remarkable language: 'dividing the two armies was wasteland, pock-marked with craters here and there broken trees and stunted willows that marked the course of innumerable swollen brooks'. Regarding his descriptions of actual battle Sidney had plenty to tell after Neuve Chapelle:

> I wrote about a "show" being likely to come off. My God! What a show! I wont forget it in a hurry…we got our instructions to be

ready for a fight in the morning. We had to get up at 2am and took up a position along a line of trenches. We were told what to expect and a terrific artillery bombardment started at 7.30. What a terrible noise. You can have no idea how it sounded.

Sidney's talent for leadership showed itself most clearly at Neuve Chapelle. During the battle he led his platoon from the British into the German trenches, told to take over and not move until the Colonel arrived. On walking into the German trenches, Sidney depicted the 'havoc wrought by our bombardment' in the German lines:

> The sight of those German trenches still haunt me. Standing on dead bodies all covered with blood is not much good for one after a good breakfast....not that I had had a good breakfast...but still it was awful.

However, a Sergeant from another regiment requested urgent assistance clearing about 50 Germans from part of a trench that had not yet been taken, which Sidney agreed to. On attacking the German barricade, Sidney then takes the moment to tell his parents light-heartedly: 'We picked up German helmets and tried them on!' Sidney then met the Colonel, who informed him that he had done the right thing in assisting the other regiment, and instructed Sidney's platoon to advance on another ruined house filled with Germans. In this attack, one of what Sidney referred to as 'my chaps' was killed, and two injured. Much later, on 29 April, the 'Fourth' learned that honours had been awarded to the 4th Black Watch, and that the only Military Cross awarded for gallantry in battle, as recommended by the Lieutenant-Colonel, was granted to Sidney Steven for his actions at Neuve Chapelle.

A couple of months later, Sidney also took part in the Battle of Aubers Ridge, which he claimed was 'not quite as bad as it had been at Neuve Chapelle but bad enough'. His description of the battle scenes, however, were far more graphic:

> You could hardly hear yourself speak the noise was so awful! Men were being knocked out, right and left....I can't describe it. It was too terrible. No one can have any conception of what it is like unless they have been through it...One man had his head blown off and another was screaming for a bandage. It is all too terrible to describe...I can't try.

Such descriptions were unlikely to relieve his parents of the worry they undoubtedly felt for their son, who always tried to make events as realistic as possible. He regularly admired Germans' shooting skills, stating in early April that 'if you fire a shot at their trench from one corner of your traverse you have to duck pretty quickly for as sure as death a shot will come back that way'. He continued in the same vein saying that 'in some bits of the line if you even put up your periscope above the parapet bullets will start whistling all around', detailing that in many spots where the enemy predicts men will emerge, they placed stationary guns, so all they needed to do on sight was to pull the trigger. Yet despite such descriptions, Sidney always attempted to alleviate his parents' worry which, for a time at least, was successful as he was allowed to return home on leave in early autumn 1915.

On his return, Sidney thanked his parents for 'giving me such a good time', and stated gratefully that 'I don't think I could have enjoyed myself better'. Somewhat sadly, he mentioned that 'I saw you looking for me as the train left but you were not far enough down the platform and I could not catch your eye'. Not long after this, he provided the first whiff of preparations for a large battle: 'Everybody is very busy just now...but dont [*sic*] say a word about that to anyone. I will write to you again before anything happens so dont be worried'. He later revealed that everything has gone very quiet, 'and we dare not talk of impending operations', warning his parents not to 'mention to a soul' that he had mentioned the impending 'show'. Expecting a movement any time soon, Sidney wrote:

> Things are beginning to look up and you may expect news soon in the papers from our part of the line. To tell you the truth I think we are going to be in for a very hot time of it very shortly. The Battalion is to be in an attack on the German front line one day very soon and I think there is going to be some very severe fighting. I must say I am looking forward to it. I sound a blood thirsty sort of a fiend. I only hope I come out of it without getting "pipped". If I am hit...well, I have done my best and that is all I can do. Above all, you are not to worry. I would not have told you anything about what I do if I had thought that you would.

Always one to use humour to lighten the mood, Sidney informed his parents that 'we are all very cheerful' and 'we all chaff each other about our chances'. He also notified his parents that he had heard from Harvey, who was leaving Britain to join the 4th Black Watch. Sidney explained: 'I hope he does not come out for a week or two or he might get more than he expected!' Sidney concluded this letter by alerting his parents to the fact that the mail has 'gone to pot' and that the battalion has been introduced to different Generals 'all day': factors that Sidney recognised as the inevitable prelude to an important battle. Signing off, his last words to his parents in the letter were: 'Hope you are all well.....cheerio'.

Those words were, in fact, Sidney Steven's last to his parents. He was killed at the Battle of Loos on 25 September 1915.

On 23 September, the day after Sidney wrote his final letter home, Harvey Steven wrote his first. Describing himself as being 'en route pour Roeuen (What...what!)', Harvey jovially described travelling to Le Havre and struggling to order lunch in France along with some officers of the 7th Black Watch. On 25 September, the same day the Battle of Loos began, Harvey and the other two officers with him received their orders to leave for the trenches. Harvey informed his parents that they have not seen anyone from the battalion yet, but that 'severe cannonading has been going on all along the Front. It sounds as though something is going on but we don't know what it is'. His first experiences of life in France are clearly very positive, and he signs off his first letter: '[It's] a great life and I am enjoying it so far'.

'Mother...Sid has been killed' is the first line of Harvey's next letter, dated 26 September from Merville. Revealing it was the first piece of news received upon his arrival, Harvey had been stopped by one of Sidney's men 'who told me that Sid was killed in the second line of German trenches'. After listing others familiar to his family who had been killed or wounded, including Major Tosh and Lieutenant-Colonel Harry Walker, Harvey offered consolation to his parents: 'It is all very sad reading for you but they died nobly, so please Mother, bear up and trust in Providence'. He signed off this short letter, in which it is clear that Harvey has little further information, but assures them that he is in good health and 'you can depend upon it that I will do my duty'. The next day, he wrote from the reserve trenches with more news and the story of Sidney's death:

> Sid was last seen, mortally wounded in the second line of German trenches, firing the last rounds of his revolver and killing six Boches. That is authentic. He will be reported officially missing but there can be no doubt that he has gone. What a death....

Harvey's letters are quite different to his brother's; far shorter and more to the point. He informed his parents that he was put in command of 'C' Company, which was the one Sidney led prior to his death. Indeed, the majority of Harvey's contribution to the Steven collection of letters is largely dedicated to informing his aggrieved parents of his brother's demise. After speaking to another soldier who claimed to be with his brother when he was shot, Harvey has managed to offer further details about Sidney's death:

> Sid, with his company following him, was attacking the second line of German trenches when he came upon seven Germans. The report I have is that he shot six of them with the six rounds in his revolver but the seventh shot him through the thigh. It was a ghastly wound. He applied a Field dressing but it would not go round so he stuffed the whole bandage into the wound and when he was being carried away he was hit again and killed.

Harvey assured his parents that he would answer any questions they have about Sidney's or any other man's death that he can, assuming 'I [don't] suppose you will be disappointed at hearing from me so often'. There is an indication in Harvey's letters that his parents are enquiring frequently about it, hearing rumours about Loos and Sidney's death that Harvey strives to answer. Clearly responding to a letter from his mother expressing a good deal of grief, Harvey pleaded: 'Dear mother, do not grieve but rather be proud to take so big a share in this great victory. I shall revenge the death of my pals but always with regard to my safety'. Harvey mentioned in the same letter that he received a letter from his father 'to Sid and myself', from which Harvey could deduce that 'you had evidently heard of the move by then but did not know what the cost was going to be'. In a further letter, Harvey has obviously received a letter from his parents expressing hope that Sidney may somehow still be alive since he is still at this point reported 'missing in action' and not 'killed in action':

There is one thing that I want to make quite clear. It is possible that when the casualties are reported officially, Sid may be reported as missing or wounded or something like that. You must take no notice of that because unless an officer is actually seen killed by another officer it cannot be officially reported. With so many officers gone from us there is no brother officer who saw him fall so the information rests with the men from whom I have had quite clear evidence as to how Sid died.

Taking an almost parental role in making things calmly but precisely clear about the nature of his brother's death, Harvey never provided his own feelings or point of view regarding his brother's death, but clearly cared a great deal in alleviating any pains his parents had.

When he was not reporting his brother's death, Harvey demonstrated much the same attitude as his brother to life at the Front. He also enjoyed jogging along the road with the men whilst singing heartily, telling his parents that he is fit and well. He took up Sidney's usual order of cigarettes and tobacco, and notified his parents that he went through Sidney's belongings, some of which he has sent home, whilst his clothes were distributed amongst his former Company, which Harvey described as 'a pitiful sight'. Harvey never alluded to his own feelings around his younger brother's death, but attempted to console his family: 'Mother, again I pray you to "stick it"'. The gravity of the situation comes into play when Harvey mentions that 'Sid's new tunic has arrived but it is of no use to me': only a few days before, Sidney had been complaining that the tunic he had ordered from London whilst on leave had not yet arrived.

At Givenchy, Harvey was put in charge of half of the Battalion, a task he saw as 'truly a most honourous [sic] position'. Harvey explained that the men have been in the trenches for three days and only the 2nd Black Watch have suffered a few casualties, describing a 'severe bombardment' to the right of their position. He bragged that, although 'all day big guns, little guns, machine guns and rifles have been firing away', and despite even the explosion of two mines next to their trench, he has been able to sleep through the noise. Harvey tells his parents that 'we look forward to letters like starving men long for food!' and looks forward to the "Advertiser" promised by his father, saying: 'I am anxious to read what they say in Dundee about their now famous Battalion'. Trying to cheer the tone, Harvey explained to his mother that he believed, 'if it were not all so sad', that she would laugh to see him covered 'from head to foot' in mud in the trenches. It is at this point that Harvey told his parents that: 'I am quite content with this life and I shall not mind a bit as long as it does not get any worse!' He imagined the church bells ringing at home – 'it must be just about their time as I write – and apologises for the letter being egotistical 'but I feel you would want to know all about me'. Like Sidney's letters he signs off: 'Cheerio'.

Harvey described 7 October as a 'lovely day', and willed the sun to break through into the trenches to 'dry them up rapidly' after the rainfall of early October. Harvey mentioned to his parents that 'a great deal of responsibility has been lifted off my shoulders' as he and the other officers reverted back to the rank of 2nd Lieutenant, but he did not disclose whether or not he was happy with this result. He did, however, seem to think this would make his parents feel better. Perhaps in the most sentimental and personal passage in his short collection of letters, Harvey told them:

> Mother, you ask me to take care of myself. I shall do that never fear, consistent, as I have said before with my duty. I shall do it for your sake…and probably for my own! In these last years we have realized how strictly and yet how fairly you and father have brought us up and now you have your reward in the universal love and respect that has been paid to Sid.

The newspapers were, by 7 October, mourning the loss of Harvey's brother, Sidney, the first member of the battalion to be decorated with a medal for gallantry. At the close of his letter, Harvey reported that 'tonight my boys are out repairing the parapet in front of our trench', and despite regular shelling outside, explained that 'it is time that I went along and visited them'. Harvey went out to check on his men and was almost instantly killed by a rifle grenade.

Harvey's last word in the letter to his parents was the same as his brother who died twelve days before: 'Cheerio'.

NOTES

[1] All quotations in this chapter are drawn from the letters of Sidney and Harvey Steven, Imperial War Museum, London: Documents, 5525.

Epilogue

I want very much to tell you about my comrades - great-hearted comrades - many of whom did not come home.
They wanted to be remembered, not as pale ghosts, but as honest, suffering soldier lads.

- William Linton Andrews

Whilst the 'Fourth' was going through the regrettable process of amalgamation, the newspapers in Dundee commemorated their anniversary of leaving Dundee on 23 February 1915 through the printing of letters, interviews and citizens' poetry. Although it is generally believed that the newspapers did not publish full casualty lists, *The People's Journal* published under the headline 'A YEAR'S TOLL' a list of the killed and missing soldiers of the 4th Black Watch from the time they left Dundee until almost exactly a year later. The list revealed that 112 men had officially been reported killed, but many others were missing – approximately 80 men of all ranks – and gradually confirmed dead, their names leaking into the Dundee press in ones and twos during the months of 1916. The accompanying report described 'Dundee's Heroes' as imprinting the 4th Black Watch's name in history 'with an indelible dye of blood'.[1] Much later, indeed a whole decade after the Battle of Aubers Ridge, a 'Record of the Fourth' written by Lieutenant-Colonel Muir – previously Major Muir – was published in *The People's Journal*, showing that nine officers and 403 other ranks of the 4th Black Watch had perished up to the time of the amalgamation with the 5th.[2] Although the figures revealed in early 1916 account for only half of Muir's figure, when those who died of wounds in the following years are taken into account, together with the fact that in February 1916 some details of the battles were still unknown, it appears that the newspapers simply did not have all the information available in 1915, rather than being guilty of a deliberate attempt to conceal the truth.

Examining the casualty figures suffered by the 4th Black Watch during the time it existed as an independent entity, evidence shows that the battalion suffered nearly a thousand casualties in a year, with the total number exceeding the 900 officers and men who arrived in Le Havre in February 1915. In the wider story of The Black Watch in the Great War, the 25 battalions it raised for service on all fronts apparently saw more than 50,000 men passing through the regiment during the four years of the war, of whom 28,000 were killed or wounded, and 68 battle honours won, including four Victoria Crosses.[3] Within this, the story of the 4th Black Watch, and by extension the story of Dundee's experiences of the First World War through its soldiers' words, has been told. Of course, men of Dundee in other battalions and regiments in the British Army contributed hugely to the war effort and, as has been shown throughout this book, were appreciated by the newspapers and people of Dundee. However, it was the 'Fourth' that symbolised this city's experience: the experience of a city at war.

Adrian Faber argues that 'localness is seen as crucial to understanding the First World War and provincial newspapers are an important part of that localness'.[4] The provincial press in Dundee was certainly able to present very personal accounts of soldiers' experiences at the front, particularly concerning casualties. Newspapers such as the *Dundee Advertiser* and *The Courier and Argus* could report the 4th Battalion's movements and casualties in a manner relevant to the city; an altogether more human reportage. The diversity in the newspapers of Dundee allowed readers of all classes in the city to follow the men of the 'Fourth', and the large variety of reports both by journalists and soldiers meant that consumers of the D.C. Thomson publications had little doubt what was happening to their men on the front between February 1915 and March 1916. Contrary to Pandrich's view that 'the picture presented by the newspapers was not a clear one', this study has attempted to illuminate the ability of the Dundee press to represent the 4th Black Watch for the most part in an honest manner.[5] Although sensationalism did occur, mainly in the patriotic *People's Journal*, this was not in a manner damaging to people's perceptions of the war, and was certainly not a collusive attempt to deceive the Dundee public.

This book has aimed to present, in the context of the actions of the 4th Black Watch during its existence as an independent unit in France, that the aforementioned realm of the provincial press, whilst read alongside first-hand accounts of soldiers as well as official documentation, is not only a legitimate but also a potentially rich and significant field for historical study. Leniency surrounding censorship, publication of letters depicting all manner of attitudes towards war and accurate representations of trench life presented by local newspapers have all been explored with reference to the Dundee press. As this book has demonstrated, there was an inextricable link between the soldiers and civilians that was not only represented but enhanced by the Dundee newspapers; a level of closeness which would not have been possible in a national newspaper. As mentioned, the government admitted that it could not scour the multitude of newspapers of the provincial press during the First World War. Surely this is indication enough that the last thing historians should be doing in the present day is neglecting this potentially invaluable source of gauging opinions and experiences of citizens from all classes. With the centenary of the Great War being commemorated over the coming years, historians will continue to focus on the issues surrounding the War from a modern-day perspective. The provincial press provides a unique insight into public opinion of the War as reports fluctuated between negative and positive as a direct result of its citizen soldiers' experiences. The provincial newspapers of the time also contain many telling first-hand accounts directly from those fighting on the front lines and address many contentious issues such as officer-man relationships and conscription. Although this study has been limited in discussing the wider issues readily exposable in the wartime press, now is the optimum time for a more detailed study with a broader remit to be conducted.

Building on the valuable work of Stephen Badsey and Adrian Faber, this book has, whilst ultimately telling the worthy story of the 4th Battalion The Black Watch, simultaneously aimed to highlight the fact that reportage of men at the front was not as distorted as previously assumed. This argument has been based on the personal accounts of soldiers such as Alex Thomson, Sidney and Harvey Steven, and W. L. Andrews commenting upon the accuracy of the reports in Dundee's newspapers. A further comparison between the provincial and national press across Scotland would assist scholars in understanding both the nature of the press and the variety of journalism available to citizens during the First World War. The provincial press in particular, due to its cheek-by-jowl relationship with the communities within which it reported, is undoubtedly a neglected yet readily available source that requires – and certainly deserves – further attention. In the words of Sir John Simon in his report depicting the Press Bureau as a 'whipping boy', it is time that the role of the Great War press 'was made plain'.[6]

It is somewhat unusual for a book about the First World War to concentrate on the Battles of Neuve Chapelle, Aubers Ridge and Loos, but to omit the Battle of the Somme and Passchendale. Indeed, there remains a distinct lack of work on the earlier years of the First World War, with much historiography revolving around the battles witnessed from mid-1916 onwards. Yet, despite this, the story of the 4th Black Watch was an eventful one, with many important factors that contribute to an understanding of the experience of war as seen through the eyes of soldiers. The early period of the war is certainly neglected, but should not remain so.

This book has, to some small measure, attempted to contribute to the current revisionist historiographical work being conducted at present by historians such as Gary Sheffield, Stephen Badsey and Hew Strachan to name but a few. In the 1930s, the widespread anti-war tradition that began to spread its now almost impenetrable roots into Britons' collective memory of the First World War, which culminated in the 1960s, has in a large way remained the accepted interpretation of the war. There is a tendency at present to present the soldiers of the First World War as helpless victims who, as soon as they recognised their dire circumstances, were trapped. As difficult as it may be for the modern interpreter to understand given the strong 'lions led by donkeys' culture of the twentieth century, the story of the 'Fourth' is just one example that shows very few soldiers saw their situation in this way. William Linton Andrews, Alexander Thomson, Sidney and Harvey Steven and many other voices in the newspapers, and indeed many of those who did not put their hand to journals or memoirs did not feel this way. That they did not see themselves as helpless pawns does not by any means equate to them being irrational. Andrews, a discerning and intelligent man with a profession in journalism and life after the war as a writer, acknowledged the hardships and horrors of war, but concluded of his time with the 4th and 4/5th Black Watch that it was 'the longest and in the main happiest chapter' of his life.[7] Harvey Steven, after losing his brother at the Battle of Loos and who himself died just twelve days later declared in the midst of his grief: 'I am quite content with this life'. Another soldier whose personal testament has been central to this book, Alexander Thomson, felt similarly. On finally returning home to Dundee on 6 October 1915, prior to receiving a commission and a place in the 7th Black Watch as a Captain, Thomson summed up his experience:

> Ah, well – a bath and a change and the story of my life in the ranks is ended. It is a rough story, which at the best can give but little idea what the life was really like, but I hope, should I ever forget the year 1915 and all the lessons it taught me, that these pages will, in some measure at least, bring back memories of all that is noble and good in war. The horror, the cruelty and the hardening of heart I turn from as best I can, knowing full well they are bound to leave their mark inevitably but hoping still, contrary though it seems, to draw some good from these months of contact with them.[8]

The First World War experience has remained close to the hearts of many citizens of Dundee for nearly a full century. Indeed, a physical testament to the memory of fallen soldiers from both great wars of the twentieth century dominates the skyline of the Scottish city. The Dundee Law is the city's most distinctive landmark, and the memorial erected on its summit in 1925 is dedicated to the memory of the men not only those of the 4th Black Watch, but all those in Dundee who died in the First, and latterly the Second World Wars. Dundee, a city whose reputation lies in its history of whaling, port industry, jute and flax manufacture, marmalade and journalism, is also fundamentally a city of remembrance. Each year, the beacon on the Dundee Law monument is lit on four days: first on 25 September to recognise the Battle of Loos; 24 October for United Nations Day; Armistice Day on 11 November; and Remembrance Sunday. The first day of commemoration acknowledges the battle at which so many men of Dundee, particularly concentrated in the ranks of the 4th Black Watch, lost their lives or were wounded. So intrinsic is the memory of those soldiers to the citizens of Dundee that the light, as well as the appreciation of the soldiers' efforts, carries on. Far from a bitter memory of a futile and needless loss of men, Dundee's continued appreciation of the men who died during the First World War challenges clichés, reaffirms community values and, most importantly, remembers the men who died. 25 September is, to a large and significant extent, Dundee's own Remembrance Day.

NOTES

[1]   *The People's Journal*, 23 February 1916.

[2]   *The People's Journal*, 16 May 1925.

[3]   John Parker, *Black Watch: The Inside Story of the Oldest Highland Regiment in the British Army* (London: Headline Book Publishing, 2005), pp. 173-174.

[4]   Faber, p. 6.

[5]   Pandrich, p. 124.

[6]   *The Courier and Argus*, 12 October 1915.

[7]   W. L. Andrews, *Linton Andrews: The Autobiography of a Journalist* (London: Ernest Benn Limited, 1964), p. 84.

[8]   Diary of Alex Thomson, 6 October 1915, p. 77.

Select Bibliography

Manuscripts and Periodicals

Dundee Central Library
Courier and Argus, August 1914 – April 1916.

Dundee Advertiser, February 1915 – March 1916; December 1917 – January 1918.

The People's Journal – Dundee War Memorial Supplement – 16 May 1925.

The People's Journal – 'The Dinna Forget Book of the 4th Black Watch'.

The People's Journal, July 1914 – May 1916.

The Dundee Yearbook, 1914-1916.

The Black Watch Regimental Archive
BWRA 0290 – Photograph Album of Life in the Trenches.

BWRA 0296 – Lieutenant-Colonel Harry Walker's Field Service Book.

BWRA 0441 – Official War Diary and Record of the Fourth Battalion Black Watch.

BWRA 5795 – 4th Black Watch Photograph Album.

BWRA 0712 – Diary of Captain A. B. Thomson, 4th Black Watch.

University of Dundee Archives
First World War Collection

MS 106/1/9 – Letters from Captain Patrick Duncan to his family, 1914-1918.

MS 106/2 – Letters from Private William Cuthill to his parents, 1915.

Imperial War Museum, London
Transcript of letters from Lieutenants Harvey and Sidney Steven, February - October 1915, private papers, Documents.5525.

Online Archives
The Scotsman Digital Archive, February-October 1915.

Books

Andrews, W. L., *Haunting Years* (London: Naval & Military Press Reprint, 2001) (original pub. 1930).

Andrews, W. L., *Linton Andrews: The Autobiography of a Journalist* (London: Ernest Benn Limited, 1964).

Bond, Brian & Cave, Nigel (eds.), *Haig: A Re-appraisal 70 Years On* (Barnsley: Pen & Sword Military, 1999); *Haig: A Re-appraisal 80 Years On* (Barnsley: Pen & Sword Military, 2009).

Boyce, G., Curran, J. & Wingate, P. (eds.), *Newspaper History: From the 17th Century to the Present Day* (London: Constable, 1978).

Burrows, Bob, *Fighter Writer: The Eventful Life of Sergeant Joe Lee, Scotland's Forgotten War Poet* (Derby: Breedon Books, 2004).

Cecil, Hugh & Liddle, Peter (eds.), *Facing Armageddon: The First World War Experienced* (London: Leo Cooper, 1996).

Dearle, N. B., *Dictionary of Official War-time Organizations* (London: Humphrey Milford, 1928).

DeGroot, Gerard J., *Blighty: British Society in the Era of the Great War* (New York: Addison Wesley Longman, 1996).

Ferro, Marc, *The Great War* (London: Routledge Classics, reprinted 2002) (original pub. 1974).

Hart, Liddel, *History of the First World War* (London: Pan Books Ltd. Reprint, 1972) (original pub. 1930).

Holmes, Richard, *Tommy: The British Soldier on the Western Front 1914-1918* (London: Harper Perennial, 2005).

Howard, Michael (ed.), *A Part of History: Aspects of the British Experience of the First World War* (London & New York: Continuum, 2008).

Knightley, Philip, *The First Casualty: The War Correspondent as Hero, Propagandist and Myth Maker From the Crimea to Vietnam* (London: Andre Deutsch Limited, 1975).

Lee, A. J., *The Origins of the Popular Press, 1855-1914* (London: Croom Helm, 1976).

Lee, Joseph Johnstone, *Ballads of Battle* (London: John Murray, 1916).

Linklater, Eric & Andro, *The Black Watch* (London: Barrie & Jenkins Ltd., 1977).

Macdonald, Catriona M.M. & McFarland, E.W. (eds.), *Scotland and the Great War* (East Lothian: Tuckwell Press Ltd., 1999).

Marwick, Arthur, *The Deluge*, 2nd ed. (London: Macmillan Press Ltd., 1991).

Merewether, J. W. B. & Smith, Frederick, *The Indian Corps in France*, 2nd ed. (London: John Murray, 1919).

Messinger, Gary S., *British Propaganda and the State in the First World War* (Manchester: Manchester University Press, 1992).

Parker, John, *Black Watch: The Inside Story of the Oldest Highland Regiment in the British Army* (London: Headline Book Publishing, 2005).

Ponsonby, Arthur, *Falsehood in War-Time* (USA: E.P. Dutton & Co., 1928).

Rose, Jonathan, *The Intellectual Life of the British Working Classes* (New Haven & London: Yale University Press, 2001).

Royle, Trevor, *The Flowers of the Forest* (Edinburgh: Birlinn Limited, 2006).

Sheffield, Gary, *Forgotten Victory: The First World War: Myths and Realities* (London: Headline Review, 2002).

Spear, Hilda D. & Pandrich, Bruce (eds.), *Sword and Pen: Poems of 1915 from Dundee and Tayside* (Aberdeen: Aberdeen University Press, 1989).

Taylor, A. J. P., *The First World War: An Illustrated History* (London: Penguin Books Ltd., 1966).

Taylor, Philip M., *Munitions of the Mind*, 3rd ed. (Manchester: Manchester University Press, 2003).

Wauchope, A. G., *History of the Black Watch in the Great War* (London: Naval & Military Press Reprint, 2002) (original pub. 1925).

Young, Derek, *Forgotten Scottish Voices from the Great War* (Gloucestershire: Tempus, 2005).

Journal Articles
Hopkin, Deian, 'Domestic Censorship in the First World War', *Journal of Contemporary History*, 5 (4) (1970), pp. 150-169.

Lloyd, Nick, "With Faith and Without Fear": Sir Douglas Haig's Command of First Army During 1915, *The Journal of Military History*, 71 (4) (2007), pp. 1051-1076.

McEwen, J. M., 'The National Press During the First World War: Ownership and Circulation', *Journal of Contemporary History*, 17 (1982), pp. 459-486.

Messinger, Gary, 'Truth Under Fire: War and the Media', *New England Journal of Public Policy*, 19 (2) (2005), pp. 297-315.

White, Bonnie J., 'Volunteerism and Early Recruitment Efforts in Devonshire, August 1914-December 1915', *The Historical Journal*, 52 (3) (2009), pp. 641-666.

Magazine Articles
'Narratives of the 4th, 5th, 4/5th, and 9th (16th Division) Battalions, *The Red Hackle*, October 1923, pp. 40-42.

Dissertations and Theses
Faber, Adrian, 'The Provincial Press During the First World War: A Case Study of the Wolverhampton *Express & Star* between January and March 1918, University of Birmingham Centre for First World War Studies, MA dissertation, 2006.

Pandrich, Bruce F. J., 'Dundee's Flodden: a Sociological Study through the Written Word, University of Dundee, M.Phil thesis, 1988.

Index

The Abertay Historical Society

Honorary Presidents
Lord Provost of the City of Dundee
Provost of Angus
Provost of Perth and Kinross
Principal of the University of Dundee
Principal of the University of St Andrews

President
Christina Donald

Vice-Presidents
Fiona Sinclair
David Orr

General Secretary
Matthew Jarron
c/o University of Dundee Museum Services, Dundee DD1 4HN
e-mail: museum@dundee.ac.uk

Treasurer
Dorothy Connelly
3 Viewpark Cottages
Gardner's Lane, Dundee DD1 5RE
e-mail: dorothy.connelly@btinternet.com

Book Editor
Billy Kenefick
History, School of Humanities, University of Dundee, Dundee DD1 4HN

Sales Secretary
Catherine Smith
Alder Archaeology, 55 South Methven Street, Perth PH1 5NX
e-mail: csmith@alderarchaeology.co.uk

The Society was founded in May 1947 and exists to promote interest in local history. For further information, please visit our website at **www.abertay.org.uk**

Publications of the Abertay Historical Society currently in print

No.28   Enid Gauldie, *One Artful and Ambitious Individual,*
          Alexander Riddoch (1745-1822), (Provost of Dundee
          1787-1819). (1989)
          ISBN 978 0 900019 24 1

No.35   Annette M. Smith, *The Nine Trades of Dundee.* (1995)
          ISBN 978 0 900019 31 9

No.37   Michael St John, *The Demands of the People, Dundee*
          Radicalism 1850-1870. (1997) ISBN 978 0 900019 33 3

No.39   Lorraine Walsh, *Patrons, Poverty & Profit: Organised Charity*
          in Nineteenth Century Dundee. (2000) ISBN 978 0 900019 35 7

No.41   Ian McCraw, *Victorian Dundee at Worship.* (2002)
          ISBN 978 0 900019 37 9

No.42   Andrew Murray Scott, *Dundee's Literary Lives vol 1: Fifteenth*
          to Nineteenth Century. (2003) ISBN 978 0 900019 38 7

No 43   Andrew Murray Scott, *Dundee's Literary Lives vol 2:*
          Twentieth Century. (2004) ISBN 978 0 900019 39 5

No 45   Annette M. Smith, *The Guildry of Dundee: A History of the*
          Merchant Guild of Dundee up to the 19th century. (2005)
          ISBN 978 0 900019 42 5

No 46   Mary Verschuur, *A Noble and Potent Lady: Katherine*
          Campbell, Countess of Crawford. (2006) ISBN 978 0 900019 43 2

No 47   Kenneth Cameron, *The Schoolmaster Engineer: Adam Anderson*
          of Perth & St Andrews 1780-1846. (2007)
          ISBN 978 0 900019 44 9

No 48   Sarah F. Browne, *Making the Vote Count: The Arbroath*
          Womens' Citizens Association, 1931-1945. (2007)
          ISBN 978 0 900019 45 6

No 49   Ann Petrie, *The 1915 Rent Strikes: An East Coast Perspective.*
         (2008) ISBN 978 0 900019 46 3

No 51   Matthew Jarron *et al* (editors), *Ten Taysiders: Forgotten Figures
         from Dundee, Angus and Perthshire.* (2011)
         ISBN 978 0 900019 48 7

No 52   Susan Keracher, *Dundee's Two Intrepid Ladies: A Tour Round the
         World by D.C. Thomson's Female Journalists in 1894.* (2012)
         ISBN 978 0 900019 49 4

No 53   Flora Davidson, *Glen Clova Through The Ages: A Short Guide to
         the History of an Angus Glen.* (2013)
         ISBN 978 0 900019 50 0

All publications may be obtained through booksellers or by post from the
Hon Sales Secretary, Abertay Historical Society, Alder Archaeology, 55
South Methven Street, Perth, PH1 5NX (e-mail:
csmith@alderarchaeology.co.uk)